WHATSOEVER TH

Whatsoever Things are True

CLASSIC DISCOURSES ON TRUTH

JAMES HENLEY THORNWELL

Solid Ground Christian Books
Birmingham, Alabama

Solid Ground Christian Books
2090 Columbiana Rd, Suite 2000
Birmingham, AL 35216
205-443-0311
sgcb@charter.net
http://solid-ground-books.com

Whatsoever Things are True
CLASSIC DISCOURSES ON TRUTH

James Henley Thornwell (1812-1862)

First published 1855 by Messrs. Carter, New York, NY

Solid Ground Classic Reprints

First printing of new edition May 2005

*Special thanks to Ric Ergenbright for again granting us
permission to use his photo on our cover. This image is
Lake Sakakawea, North Dakota, and can be found at
Ric's website www.ricergenbright.com*

Cover work by Borgo Design, Tuscaloosa, AL
Contact them at nelbrown@comcast.net

ISBN: 1-932474-78-1

Author's Preface

This unpretending little volume consists of a series of Discourses preached in the ordinary routine of the author's ministrations as Chaplain of the South Carolina College. He has ventured to publish them, because the young men who heard them thought that they derived benefit from them; and as the subject is eminently adapted to the case of the youthful student, it did not seem presumptuous to hope that what had been useful here might also be productive of good beyond the walls of the college. The times require some such discussion as that which is here attempted. The author is by no means sanguine, however, of any other success than that which may be found in the cordial approbation of his own pupils. They will accept the work in the spirit in which it has been written; and if it shall have the effect of imbuing their minds with that generous love of truth which constitutes the noblest inspiration of the scholar—if it shall lead them to Him who is the Fountain of truth, and to the study of that eternal Word which is the only infallible message of truth—he will feel that he has not labored in vain, whatever reception his little manual may experience at the hands of strangers and critics.

The structure of the sermons may be explained by the circumstance that the author sustains the double office in the College of a Preacher of the Gospel and a Teacher of Moral Philosophy. It is his custom to make the pulpit and the lecture-room subservient to each other. With these brief statements he sends the book into the world to speak for itself, and he earnestly prays that He whose prerogative alone it is to bless, and who can accomplish the purposes of His grace as well by the feeblest as the mightiest instrument, may make it speak with power to the understandings and consciences of all into whose hands it may chance to come.

J. H. Thornwell

DISCOURSES ON TRUTH

DISCOURSE I — THE ETHICAL SYSTEM OF THE BIBLE

Design of the discussion to determine what there is in the domain of ethics peculiar to revelation, and what is the real nature and extent of our obligations to the Bible. Thus there may be attained a just estimate of secular morality and a proper appreciation of the Gospel. I. As to the simple knowledge of duty there may be on the one hand an exaggeration of the necessity of revelation, and on the other of the sufficiency of reason. The spheres of revelation and reason distinguished. II. The superior efficiency of the Bible as teaching duty with greater certainty, and enforcing it by motives of greater power. III. The Bible as unfolding the scheme of redemption goes still farther: it teaches lessons new and distinctively its own which are unknown to philosophy. 1. It sheds new light upon the doctrine of Happiness. This exemplified by a comparison of the teaching of the Bible as to the nature of happiness with that of Aristotle. 2. It is singular in its doctrine of Holiness. The nature of holiness. 3. It furnishes the only satisfactory answer to the question, "How shall man accomplish the end of his being?" That answer is, "The provision of a method by which a double work is supernaturally effected: first, a change in man's judicial relations; secondly, a change in the temper and disposition of his soul." *1*

DISCOURSE II —THE LOVE OF TRUTH

The purpose of this discussion, to show that the love of truth as a regulative law of the whole man ought to attach to the processes of the understanding and the formation of opinions. The doctrine of the Scriptures is that the domain of morality extends to the whole man, including the understanding. 1. The will has jurisdiction over the whole man. The springs of action directed to the mind, especially curiosity, have an ethical character as coming under the jurisdiction of the will. 2. It is the prerogative of truth alone to invigorate the mind. 3. The intimate connection between the moral and intellectual natures renders lubricity of principle a consequent of confusion of the understanding as to truth. The theory discussed that the faculty which distinguishes between truth and falsehood is the same which distinguishes between right and wrong. 4. The love of truth is the general habit of mind, of which honesty, frankness, sincerity and faithfulness are only specific manifestations. Examination of the objection to these views that the operations of the mind in the department of speculative truth are exempt from the authority of the will. Mackintosh, Brougham. Men responsible for their opinions, because responsible—1. For the motives which influence their mental operations, and 2. For the circumstances which give direction to them. Practical conclusion: the obligation to make truth for its own sake the great end of intellectual effort *24*

Table of Contents

DISCOURSE III —THE LOVE OF TRUTH

All men not bound to know all truth. But in the inquiries in which each man is engaged he is bound to seek nothing but truth. Each man is bound to seek that degree of knowledge which is necessary to furnish him for his particular sphere of duty. The design of this discussion is to point out the nature of the love of truth, and some of the prominent difficulties which hinder the pursuit of truth. Commendation of Locke's view that the mind should be in a state of indifference as to what upon honest inquiry shall prove to be truth. The great and comprehensive law for the conduct of the understanding, that evidence is the measure of assent, expounded. The primary data of consciousness the standard and measure of evidence. The ways in which we are liable to be misled: first, in mistaking other things for these original data; secondly, in misapplying these data themselves. In the first, a wrong standard of judgment is assumed; in the second, a right standard is improperly used. To these two heads all prejudice ultimately referable. Specimens of these false methods. Importance of the principle that evidence is the measure of assent. Necessity of maintaining to this end liberty of discussion. The right temper of controversy. The danger resulting from the influence of vanity upon the pursuit of truth. Similar danger from the influence of the sense of shame *44*

DISCOURSE IV — SINCERITY

Two leading aspects of truth—speculative and practical. Practical truth includes three things: sincerity, faithfulness, consistency. The matter of veracity twofold—immediate and remote. I. The grounds of the obligation of veracity discussed. Views of Paley and Whewell criticised. The real ground affirmed. II. The modes in which the law of sincerity is to be applied. 1. Application not to speech alone, but to all the signs of thought. 2. Application of the law in the case of parables, fictions, tales and figurative language. 3. Application of the law to what may be called interrogatories by action. 4. Application of the law to cases of silence, or partial and evasive information. III. Modes in which the law of sincerity is evaded, or deceit practiced. 1. Vain-boasting and self-disparagement. 2. Flattery. 3. Pretensions to a friendship which is not felt. 4. Equivocation. 5. Mental reservations, when what is suppressed is not obvious from the circumstances, or is not necessary to prevent deception. IV. The question of the justifiableness of lying under any circumstances discussed *67*

DISCOURSE V — FAITHFULNESS

The Definition of the term and the thing. Three heads which embrace Faithfulness—Promises, Pledges, Vows. I. Definition of Promises. Defective definition criticized. Distinction between apparent and real promises. Elements involved in true definition. 1. Any mode of voluntary signification, without limitation to any particular class of signs. 2. The signification must be voluntary. 3. The signification must have a known tendency to excite expectation. 4. The signification must be in regard to a

Table of Contents

matter which is possible and right. II. The ground of the obligation of promises. 1. The law of sincerity requires a correspondence of the signification to the mental purpose. 2. The same law requires a correspondence between words and the reality of things. 3. A promise creates a right to the fulfillment of the expectation it excites. No right created by promises to do unlawful or impossible things. Two questions of casuistry: 1. Are extorted promises binding? 2. Does an unlawful condition invalidate a promise? Paley's and Whewell's views criticized. Concluding remarks as to the promises of the Gospel. PLEDGES. Definition. Honour pawned by the pledge. Guilt and injury involved in the violation of pledges. The sacredness of the pledge can never justify wrongdoing in carrying it out. God's condescension in the use of pledges to man. Cautions in regard to the thoughtless making of promises *91*

DISCOURSE VI — VOWS

Different estimate of vows by Protestants and Romanists. I. The nature of vows. 1. They are of the general nature of promises. 2. They are distinguished from other promises by the party to whom they are made—God. They thus become—(1.) Acts of worship. (2.) Oaths. This determines the nature of their matter and the spirit in which they should be made. Cautions against profaneness drawn from the matter of vows: 1. If they respect an act specifically religious, it must be appointed in God's Word. 2. If they respect an act not specifically religious, it must be either the elicit or imperate one of some virtue. 3. The matter should be in our power either according to nature or grace. II. The utility of vows. The expediency of making them. The whole question dependent upon the spirit in which they are made. 1. If they are made in the spirit of bribes, they are insults to God and injuries to us. 2. If they are regarded as possessing merit, their usefulness is destroyed. 3. Proper vows made in the right spirit are helps to piety. (1.) They strengthen the general bonds of duty. (2.) They increase the sense of union with God. (3.) They contribute to the habit of specific virtues, and so fortify the general principle of integrity. Calvin's four ends of vows. Vows not to be made common. III. The obligation of vows. Paley's view refuted. True ground of their obligation. 1. As promises to God they are binding on the ground of truth and justice. 2. As oaths, on the principle of reverence. Magnitude of the sin of vow-breach. Practical reflections suggested by the discussion *117*

DISCOURSE VII — CONSISTENCY

Primary import of the term. By a natural accommodation of its primary import consistency embraces three things—stability of opinion, harmony of life, and propriety of behavior. Consistency a virtue only when we have begun well. I. Stability of opinion. 1. This species of consistency not incompatible with all change. The love of truth the regulative principle by which all opinions are to be tested. The cause of fickleness of opinion. 2. Consistency not to be confounded with obstinacy. Distinction between them. Consistency the mean between bigotry and spurious charity. Stability of

Table of Contents

opinion never the result of direct effort. Necessity of discipline of thought as a guard against that fickleness of opinion which springs from weakness of understanding. Moral and religious culture the antidote to that fickleness which results from dishonest motives. II. Harmony of life. 1. Consideration of that species of inconsistency of life which arises from defect of the understanding—fickleness. 2. Consideration of the inconsistency which springs from defect of will—weakness. 3. The inconsistency occasioned by defect of honesty—hypocrisy. The conduct of men as to religion chargeable with inconsistency in all these aspects. III. Propriety of behavior or decorum. The obligation to make our actions correspond to our external circumstances and incidental relations. To this are necessary sensibility to beauty and moral culture. This species of consistency to be maintained in our relaxations and amusements. Appeals to the young to cultivate consistency *142*

DISCOURSES ON TRUTH.

DISCOURSE I.

THE ETHICAL SYSTEM OF THE BIBLE.

THE passage from which the text is taken gives us an enumeration of the principal duties of morality. The Apostle has been supposed to refer to the different systems which were discussed in the schools of Greek philosophy, analogous to those which have divided the inquirers of modern times. It is remarkable that his language admits of an easy application to the prominent theories of Virtue which have been proposed in Europe within the last two centuries. One, for example, places it essentially in conformity with truth; another in beauty, corresponding perhaps to the Apostle's honesty; another in obedience to nature and reason; another in disinterested benevolence; and others still in a comprehensive prudence. Similar theories obtained among the ancients. Aristotle and Plato have been reproduced in the speculations of Clarke, Cudworth and Price, the Epicureans and Sophists in the Utilitarians, and the Stoics in Butler, Reid and Stewart. The import of the Apostle's advice, upon the supposition that he refers to these disputes, is interpreted to be: Think upon these speculations, bring them to the standard of the Divine testimony, try them by the doctrines which I have taught you, and whatsoever they contain in keeping with the genius and temper of Christianity, that appropriate and practise; prove all things; hold fast that which is good.

Ingenious and plausible as this exposition appears to be, it is not, I apprehend, sustained by the context. It is rather the dictate of fancy than the result of sober and unbiassed criticism. The design of the Apostle, it rather seems to me, was to recapitulate several prominent heads of duty—to single out certain great characteristics of virtue, and to recommend everything in which these characteristics were found. He is giving the outlines of an exemplary man, and accordingly seizes upon the fundamental elements of morality—those data of consciousness which every system must acknowledge, which constitute the touchstone and standard of all speculations upon right—and inculcates as duty everything in which these elements essentially enter as constituents. The first is Truth—*whatsoever things are true.* He assumes the inherent rectitude of veracity, its indispensable and eternal obligation, and enjoins upon his readers to cultivate a spirit that shall reverence and exemplify this obligation in the whole extent of its application. He next signalizes Dignity of character, the principle of self-respect, which saves a man from the contempt of his fellows by protecting him from all that is little, or mean, or indecent in deportment—*whatsoever things are honest;* rather, whatsoever things are venerable or truly honourable—whatsoever is calculated to command respect or deserves veneration and esteem. Then comes the master-principle of Justice, or righteousness, without which all pretensions to integrity are vain and unmeaning; this is the solid basis of an upright character—*whatsoever things are just.* It is not enough, however, that our words and actions should be exempt from censure; the heart must be kept with all diligence, the streams must be healed at the fountain. The Apostle accordingly, as his Master had done before him, insists upon inward purity, the regulation of the thoughts, appetites and affections, so as to prevent the contamination of aught that is unholy or defiling—*whatsoever things are pure.* Under this head are obviously included Temperance, Chastity and Modesty. The things that are *lovely* comprehend everything that is fitted to conciliate or express the sentiment of affection and esteem. It embraces such duties as Benevolence, Urbanity, Courtesy, Affability and Sweetness of temper; whatever, in other words, springs from love in us and generates love in others. The things of *good report*, I am inclined to think, have reference to those matters, indifferent in themselves, by means of which we can recommend our persons and our cause to the confidence and goodwill of others. They not only require the ordinary duties of Politeness, but exact compliance with innocent customs and harmless prejudices where a failure to comply would expose us to unjust censures. They exclude repulsive Austerity and studied singularity of manner, and every species of Affectation or pretension. Here ends the specific enumeration; but as there might be virtues which are included under none of these heads, the Apostle, that he may omit nothing, extends his injunction to them. *If there be any virtue, and if there be any praise*—if there be anything which a good man ought to observe, anything right or praiseworthy, that cannot be reduced to any of these categories—it is to receive the Christian man's attention. His religion comprehends all duty.

This passage, then, according to the interpretation which has been given, exhibits the model of character which Christianity proposes to its followers, and which their Christian profession exacts of them that they shall steadily endeavour to realize. It is the Apostle's picture of an exemplary man.

As a specimen of the richness and compass of Scripture morality I shall single out the duty of *Truth*, and make it the subject of a series of discourses. Before entering upon them, however, I deem it not unimportant to make a few remarks upon the ethical teachings of the Scriptures, with a view to determine what there is that is peculiar to revelation, and what is the real nature and extent of our obligations to the Bible. This will lead us to a just estimate of secular morality, and perhaps impress us with a deeper sense of the priceless value of the Gospel. It is precisely because they do not comprehend the ethical relations of Christianity that many of the educated men of the country undervalue its importance. If asked what it is, and what it proposes to do for men, and what kind of offices it exacts from them, it is amazing how crude and ill-digested their notions would oftentimes appear to be.

I. So far as the simple knowledge of duty is concerned, we may err, on the one hand, by exaggerating the necessity of revelation, and on the other by exaggerating the sufficiency of reason. There can be no doubt that morality is a subject which falls within the province of natural light. To say that we are dependent on the Word and Oracle of God, as Bacon seems to insinuate,[1] "not only in those points which concern the great mysteries of the Deity, of the creation, of the redemption, but likewise those which concern the law moral truly interpreted"—to say that we can have, from the dictates of conscience, only negative conceptions of rectitude "sufficient to check the vice, but not to inform the duty"—is to contradict alike the testimony of Scripture and the experience of mankind. "For when the Gentiles, which have not the law, do by nature the things contained in the law, these having not the law are a law unto themselves." A being without the sense of obligation and a spontaneous recognition of the fundamental differences of right and wrong could not be responsible. He could not form the remotest notion of duty, and the language of authority and law might as well be addressed to stocks and stones. The elemental principles of right, therefore, which are involved in the very conception of a moral nature, must be conceded to man as man. They are the birth-rights of his being, and not the legacy of a subsequent revelation. An intelligent creature without primitive beliefs to determine and regulate the operations of the cog-

[1] Advancement of Learning. Works, vol. ii., p. 300.—*Montagu.*

nitive faculties would be no greater absurdity than a moral and responsible creature without primitive laws of right to determine and regulate the operations of moral judgment. But it is equally an error to maintain that, because the Scriptures presuppose the moral constitution of man, they are of little or no importance considered as a *rule* of life. It is one thing to say that reason is a law, and another to say that it is a perfect law. In our present fallen condition it is impossible to excogitate a standard of duty which shall be warped by none of our prejudices, distorted by none of our passions and corrupted by none of our habits. We are liable to as great perversions of the original principles of right as of the original principles of truth. The elements of reason have no power to secure their just application. There never has appeared an absolutely perfect rule of duty among any nations, however civilized and cultivated, that were destitute of Revelation. It is only of the law of the Lord as contained in the Scriptures that we can justly say, It is perfect. There are two respects in which every natural system of morality is likely to be found wanting. In the first place, the difficulty of reproducing in reflection the spontaneous processes of conscience, and of seizing upon its fundamental laws in their integrity and completeness, renders it next to impossible that the verbal generalizations of philosophy shall exactly represent the operations of the mind. Something is apt to be omitted or added. The danger is enhanced by the difficulty of distinguishing betwixt prejudices of education and natural principles; it is easy to confound a crotchet with a principle, to make a maxim of a habit of thought. In the next place, the application of these fundamental laws, supposing them properly eliminated, to the concrete cases of life requires great delicacy and caution. We are as likely to go wrong from misapplying a true principle as from adopting a false one. The heathen father admits the great law of parental affection; he misapplies it when he murders his infant child to save him from the miseries of life. The heathen son

recognizes the duty of filial piety; he reasons badly upon
it when he puts his aged parents to death. Here our
depravity exerts its power; it is a constant temptation to
pervert the original principle of right, to make light darkness and darkness light. It is here, too, that the principal
defects of every natural scheme of morality are exhibited.
True principles are falsely applied. We make crimes of
duties and duties of crimes. It is not so much that the law
is wrong, that the prime data are questionable—though they
are often defective—as that the law is not legitimately carried out; its proper applications are not seen; limitations
and exceptions are superinduced by our circumstances, and
we envelop ourselves in a cloud, and the result is that a deceived heart turns us aside. The Scriptures, as an authoritative rule of duty, guard against these defects. They prescribe the law in its fullness and integrity, they illustrate
its application by description and example, they indicate
the prejudices which are likely to pervert us, and signalize
the spirit which will always ensure obedience. By the
infallibility of their results they are of inestimable value
to the moral philosopher himself. When his speculations
contradict their statements, he knows that there is an error
in his processes; he retraces his steps and continues to renew
his investigations until he discovers the secret of his mis-
carriage. They serve the same purpose to him which the
answer to its sum serves to the child in learning his arith-
metic. They are at once a guide and a check to his
speculations. Paley[1] has depreciated the sufficiency of the
Scriptures as a rule, from the absurd notion that if they
were admitted to be complete they would dispense with the
use of moral philosophy. He took it for granted that the
sole business of philosophy was to furnish rules, and of
course, if they are already furnished to our hands, there is
no need for its investigations. To save, therefore, the credit
of the science which he had undertaken to expound, he has
impugned the value of the ethical teachings of the Bible.

[1] Moral and Political Philosophy, Book i., chap. 4.

His argument is curious. He has very singularly confounded moral philosophy with the moral·constitution of man, and because the Scriptures "presuppose, in the persons to whom they speak, a knowledge of the principles of natural justice"—that is, because they presuppose a conscience or a sense of the fundamental differences of right and wrong—he gravely concludes that they exact of men, in order to be understood, some tincture of philosophy. But it is one thing to be a moral agent, and quite another to be a moral philosopher. The Scriptures certainly expect that those to whom they speak are possessed of those principles of practical common sense without which their instructions are utterly unmeaning and absurd. But to possess these principles is not to be a philosopher. Philosophy implies reflection, speculation; it is thought questioning the spontaneous processes of mind, thought returning upon itself and seeking the nature, authority and criterion of its own laws. A man may have all that Dr. Paley ascribes to him without having once reflected upon this mysterious furniture, or asked himself a single question which properly belongs to the domain of philosophy. The Scriptures consequently, in prescribing an adequate and perfect rule of life, are far from dispensing with speculation. They leave untouched its peculiar work. The moral nature, in its phenomenal variety and essential unity, still invites the researches of the curious, and the more it is studied the more conspicuous will appear the absolute sufficiency of the Bible. The law of the Lord is perfect.

II. The superior efficiency of the Bible is universally conceded by all who admit a revelation at all. It teaches duty with greater certainty, and enforces it by motives of greater power. Dr. Paley thinks this the great merit of the Scriptures; and that it is a merit of incalculable importance will at once appear by reflecting on the tendency of temptation to blind the mind to the truth of the law or the danger of the consequences. Whatever certifies the rule or illustrates the misery of disobedience, assaults temptation in its stronghold and strips transgression of its favourite plea. The certainty of the law is put beyond question in the Scriptures, because it rests upon the immediate authority of God. It is not a deduction of reason to be questioned, but a Divine command to be obeyed. The power of the sanctions is found in the unlimited control which He who promulgates the law possesses of the invisible world. The legal motives of the Scriptures are projected on a scale of inconceivable grandeur. The Bible deals with the vast, the awful, the boundless. If it addresses our hopes and proposes the prospect of future happiness, it is an exceeding, an eternal weight of glory it dispenses. Does it remind us of a judgment to come? God is the Judge, earth and hell the subjects, angels spectators, and the complexion of eternity the doom. Does it address our fears? It reminds us of a worm that never dies, a fire that is never quenched, the blackness of darkness for ever. It is a grand system; it springs from the bosom of an infinite God and opens a field of infinite interests. Eternity is the emphasis it gives to its promises, the terror it imparts to its curse. Conscience, under the tuition of nature, may dread the future; it is the prerogative of revelation alone to lay it bare. Conscience may tremble, but revelation alone can show how justly its fears have been excited. Hence the Bible is without a rival when it speaks in the language of command. It wields the thunder of infinite power, as well as utters the voice of infinite righteousness. Still, its mightiest sanctions are not what may be called its legal motives. The scheme of redemption, in its conception and evolution, is a sublime commentary upon the sacredness and supremacy of right, which, while it reveals the ineffable enormity of sin, presents the character of God in such an aspect of venerable grandeur that Holiness becomes awful and majestic, and we insensibly adore under the moral impression which it makes. He that stands beneath the Cross and understands the scene dares not sin; not because there is a hell beneath him or an angry God above him, but because Holiness is felt to reign there—the ground on which he treads is sacred, the glory of the Lord encircles him, and, like Moses, he must remove the shoes from his feet. The Cross is a venerable spot. I love to linger around it, not merely that I may read my title to everlasting life, but that I may study the greatness of God. I use the term advisedly. God never appears to be so truly great, so intensely holy, as when, from the pure energy of principle, He gives Himself, in the person of His Son, to die, rather than that His character should be impugned. Who dares prevaricate with moral distinctions and talk of death as a greater evil than dishonour, when God, the mighty Maker, died rather than that truth or justice should be compromised? Who, at the foot of Calvary, can pronounce sin to be a slight matter? Here, then, lies the most impressive sanction of revelation. Not content to promulgate the law with absolute certainty, to put under tribute the whole resources of the invisible world, to lay its hand upon eternity and make heaven and hell its ministers, it rises yet higher and seeks to impress us with a subduing sense of the sacredness of right—to make us feel how awful goodness is; it reveals its inherent greatness, unveils its ineffable glory. It does not describe it, but shows it; and we return from the Cross with emotions similar to those of Moses when the name of the Lord was proclaimed, and the goodness of the Lord passed before him in the cleft of the rock. It is the scheme of redemption which crowns the ethical teachings of the Bible. The lesson is sealed at the Cross; there, and there only, do we shudder at sin for its own sake, and reverence right for itself.

III. But, impressive as the general truths of morality are rendered by the tragedy of redemption, that would be an inadequate view of the extent of its contributions which should stop at this point. It goes beyond the giving certainty and power to the doctrines of nature. It teaches lessons, and lessons of incalculable value, which philosophy could never have dreamed of. It opens a new chapter in the book of Ethics, and invites us to speculations as refreshing by their novelty as they are invigorating by their truth.

It is not sufficiently recollected that the doctrines of the Scriptures in relation to the destiny of man, the nature of Holiness and the means of grace are answers to the very questions which were earnestly and anxiously agitated in the schools of ancient wisdom, and which the sages of Greece and Rome proved themselves incompetent to solve. I am ashamed to add that they are answers which multitudes, with the Bible in their hands, have failed to comprehend, and have consequently been left to grope, as if struck by judicial blindness, in a thicker darkness than ever enshrouded the gifted minds of Paganism. There is a tenfold nearer approximation to the teachings of the Bible in Aristotle than there is in Paley; more affinity with the Gospel in Cicero than in the whole tribe of utilitarians.

1. First, in regard to Happiness, which is universally conceded to be the chief good of man, the conceptions of the Scriptures are noble and exalted. The nearest approximation which has been made by unassisted reason to their doctrine is in the philosophy of Aristotle. He failed to compass the whole truth only because man by wisdom cannot find out God. He saw enough, however, to impress us with a sense of the greatness of his genius, and to make us feel that, even amid the ruins of the Fall, there are yet traces of our ancient grandeur and dim foreshadowings of our future glory. He has taught us enough to make us accept joyfully those fuller disclosures of the Bible which illuminate what in him and nature is dark, and "what is low raise and support."

I do not know that I can set the benefit of revelation in a clearer light than by sketching the doctrine of Aristotle, pointing out its defects, and contrasting the whole truth with the miserable sentiments which prevail, to the corruption of society and the degradation of the age in which we live. His fundamental notion is, that Happiness consists in virtuous energies—that it is not mere pleasure, not the gratification which results from the possession of an object congruous to our desires. That is good only in a very subordinate sense which simply ministers to enjoyment. The chief good must be something pursued exclusively for its own sake, and never for the sake of anything else; it can never be used as an instrument; it must be perfect and self-sufficient. What, then, is the highest good of man? To answer this question, says Aristotle, we must understand the proper business of man as Man. · As there is a work which pertains to the musician, the statuary, the artist, which constitutes the good or end of his profession, so there must be some work which belongs to man, not as an individual, not as found in such and such circumstances and relations, but belongs to him absolutely as Man. Now, what is this? It must be something which springs from the peculiarities of his nature, and which he cannot share with the lower orders of being. It cannot, therefore, be life, for plants have that; neither can it be the pleasures of sensitive existence, for brutes have them. It must be sought in the life of a being possessed of reason; and as that can be contemplated in a twofold aspect, either as a state or as an exercise, as the possession of faculties or the putting forth of their activities, we must pitch upon the more important, which is activity or energy, or, as he also styles it, *obedience to reason.* Energy, therefore, according to reason, is characteristic of man. This is his business, and he who pursues it best is the best man. Human good, or the good of man as Man, is consequently energy according to the best and most perfect virtue.

This is a brief outline of what I regard as one of the finest discussions in the whole compass of ancient philosophy.[1] The notion is predominant that Happiness implies the perfection of our nature, and that perfection not so much in the habits considered as so many states, as in the unimpeded exercise of the faculties themselves. The being properly exerted is their good. Happiness, therefore, is not something imparted to the soul from without; it springs from the soul itself—it is the very glow of its life. It is to the mind

[1] Nichom. Ethics, Lib. i., c. 7.

what health is to the body—the regular and harmonious action of all the functions of the frame. It is not a gratification, not the pleasure which results from the correspondence between an object and a faculty; it is the very heat and fervour of spiritual life. All this is strikingly in accordance with the doctrine of Scripture. Happiness there, too, is represented as consisting in moral perfection, and moral perfection in virtuous energies. It is a well of water within the man, springing up to everlasting life. It is treated as an image of the blessedness of God; and when we remember the ceaseless activity of the Divine nature—*my Father worketh hitherto and I work*—there cannot be a more convincing proof that felicity consists in energies. To be happy is not to be torpid; it is not a state of indolent repose nor of the passive reception of extraneous influences. It is to be like God, who never slumbers nor sleeps, who fainteth not, neither is weary. This is the great thought of the Bible. The defect of Aristotle lies in this, that he has not explained how these virtuous energies are to be elicited and sustained in a course of unimpeded action. We cannot think without thinking something; we cannot love, we cannot praise, we cannot exercise any virtuous affection, without exercising it upon something. An abstraction wants life, and finite objects limit, condition and obstruct our energies. Besides this, as we shall subsequently see, the fundamental principle of virtue is love, and love implies the existence of a person with whom we are united in intimate fellowship. Communion is indispensable to the energy of Holiness, and that the energy may be unimpeded the person with whom we are in union must be worthy of the intensest affections of which we are susceptible. He must himself be the perfect Good. Now, the Scriptures propose the fellowship of God as the consummation of felicity. We may concentrate upon Him all the faculties of our nature. He can evoke their intensest activities, give them full scope and never put a period to their flow. " His favour is life, and His loving-kindness better than life. I shall be satisfied when I awake in Thy likeness." That man's chief end is to glorify God and enjoy Him for ever—that this and this only is Happiness; that we enjoy as we glorify; that the very going forth of our energies upon Him, the ever-blessed, is itself blessedness,—this is the doctrine which lies at the basis of the ethical system of the Gospel. It is a doctrine which philosophy never could have discovered, but which it pronounces to be just as soon as the terms are understood. We are so familiar with the statement of it, we have it so often on our lips or hear it so often from the desk, that we do not enter into the depth of meaning it contains. In itself it is a grand thought, a noble and exalted privilege. Fellowship with God! the real communion of our minds with His! —what tongue can express it? what heart adequately conceive it? And yet this honour have all the saints. It is not a figure, not a flourish of rhetoric, no dream of the mystic. It is a great fact; and in reflecting upon it I have often been impressed with the words of a dying saint: "Preach it at my funeral, publish it at my burial, that the Lord converses familiarly with man." His secret is indeed with them that fear Him, and He will show them His covenant. How coarse and degrading, by the side of this doctrine, do those views of Happiness appear which make it consist in pleasure! which, instead of setting man upon the improvement of himself, the perfection of his nature and the expansion of his energies in communion with God, send him in quest of the beggarly elements of earth, which all are to perish in the using! There cannot be a greater obstruction to the pursuit of real happiness than the love of pleasure. It relaxes and debilitates the mind, destroys the tone of the spirit, superinduces languor upon all the faculties; it is the grave of energy. Hence is that of Scripture: She that liveth in pleasure is dead while she liveth. If Happiness is an adumbration of the blessedness of God—and it must be so—if it is the glory of man to bear the image of God, the whole subject is manifestly degraded when it is reduced to the analogy of the enjoyment of a brute. Take the account which is given by Paley,[1] and Happiness consists not only in a succession of pleasurable sensations, but sensations immediately connected with the body. It is a sort of tickling in the region of the heart. He openly declares, too, that there is no essential difference among pleasures but that of intensity and continuance. The main thing is enjoyment; and so a man enjoys himself, he need ask no further question. The superiority of the soul to the body; the coarseness of some and the excellence of other pleasures; the dignity and refinement of moral, intellectual and spiritual gratifications, —all this is idle declamation. He that scratches with the itch experiences as noble satisfaction as he that rejoices in charity or whose soul turns upon the poles of truth! This fundamental error, that Happiness is pleasure, pervades society. It is the animating spirit of the eager and restless struggle for wealth, honour and power. It is the grand delusion of sin—a delusion whose potent spell no experience has been able to dissolve, no reasoning to dissipate. It is the vanity of the carnal heart; " every age renews the inquiry after an earthly felicity; the design is entailed and reinforced with as great a confidence and vigour as if none had been baffled or defeated in it before."[2] Philanthropy projects upon it its visionary schemes for the benefit of the race, and, forgetting that all real improvement must begin within, directs its assaults upon the outward and accidental —aims its blows at the social fabric, and seeks to introduce an order of things which shall equally distribute the sources of enjoyment. Let all men be equally rich is the insidious fallacy—equally fed, equally clothed, equally exalted in social and political condition—and, like cattle in the same pasture, they must all be equally happy. " What serious heart doth not melt and bleed for miserable men that are (through a just Nemesis) so perpetually mocked with shadows, cheated with false, delusive appearances, infatuated and betrayed by their own senses! They walk but in a vain show, disquieting

[1] Moral and Political Philosophy, Book i., chap. 6.
[2] Howe's Blessedness of the Righteous, chap. xi.

themselves in vain ; their days flee away as a shadow ; their
strength is only labour and sorrow ; while they rise up early
and lie down late to seek rest in trouble and life in death." [1]
Behold, I show you a more excellent way : fear God and
keep His commandments ; for this is the whole of man ; this
is his being's end and aim.

2. Intimately connected with the subject of Happiness is
that of Holiness. As happiness is an image of the blessedness, so holiness is an image of the moral perfections, of
God. It is, consequently, that in the energies of which
Happiness must essentially consist. It is God's likeness
that fits us to see His face. It is therefore a matter of the
very last importance that we should know what Holiness is,
or, if incomprehensible in its essence, that we should understand its phenomena and relations. It is only from the
Bible that we can obtain any satisfactory light upon these
points. Philosophy can discourse of virtues—virtues in
the habit and virtues in the act ; it can classify and arrange
the duties they exact ; but when the question arises as to the
unity of rectitude, it is utterly unable to answer. Truth is
right, justice is right, benevolence is right, temperance
is right ; the habits which prompt to the observance of
these virtues are right ; but are all these one and the same
right ? If one, in what does their unity consist ? The
actions of truth are certainly different from those of temperance ; the actions of benevolence are as clearly different from those of justice ; the habits are obviously so many
different subjective states. Where, then, is the unity, and
why is the same term applied in common to them all ?
Philosophy can only dissect consciousness, and consciousness
can only reveal to us the primitive cognitions of the moral
faculty which the constitution of our nature compels us to
accept as the criteria of right. Philosophy, consequently,
can give no other answer to the question than that all these
things, though various in themselves, receive a common
name in consequence of a common relation to conscience.

[1] Howe's Blessedness of the Righteous, chap. xi.

They are all commanded by it. As truth is essentially conformity with the laws of the understanding, so virtue is essentially conformity with the laws of conscience. Here philosophy stops. Beyond consciousness it cannot penetrate; and though it may surmise that there is a higher unity in which all these laws are ultimately grounded, it is unable to lay its hand upon it and bring it to light. Here the Scriptures come in with their doctrine of Holiness, and what philosophy had surmised they abundantly confirm. What, then, is Holiness? It is not a single habit; it is not a complement of habits; it is a NATURE, and by *nature* we are to understand, not the collection of properties which distinguish one being from another, but a generic disposition which determines, modifies and regulates all its activities and states—the law of its mode of existence. It is that out of which habit grows, from which every single action ultimately proceeds. There is a nature in the lion, the dog, the tiger, which determines their manner of life—a nature in all beings which makes them as they are. Without it there could be no character, no habits, no consistent operations. All action would be fortuitous and arbitrary. In itself we cannot define it, belonging as it does to that class of things which, incomprehensible in themselves and incapable of being represented in thought, are yet matters of necessary belief. But as there are, within the sphere of our daily experience, various generic dispositions each of which serves as the basis of very different habits, there is nothing incredible in supposing that there may be one great central disposition in which all others are grounded. The general temper of Sadness has numberless manifestations; the same is true of Joy; and there may be a temper or tone of mind in which all virtuous activities are united. To illustrate the all-pervading influence of Holiness as a nature, the Scriptures employ the striking analogy of *life*. When we ask the question, What is life? we soon become sensible that we are dealing with a subject that eludes the capacity of thought. We cannot seize it in itself; we see its effects, we witness its operations, we can mark the symptoms which distinguish its presence, but the thing itself no mortal mind can apprehend.   We can only speak of it as the unknown cause of numberless phenomena which we notice.   Where is life? Is it here and not there?   Is it there and not here?   Is it in the heart, the head, the hands, the feet?   It evidently pervades the man; it is the condition, the indispensable condition, of the organic action of every part of the frame.   The body may be perfect in its structure: it may have every limb, and nerve, and muscle, and foreign influences may be made to mimic the operations of life; but if life be not there, these actions, or rather motions, are essentially distinct from those of the living man.   In like manner Holiness pervades the soul.   Though not a habit, nor a collection of habits, it is the indispensable condition of them all.   It is not here nor there, but is diffused through the whole man—the understanding, the will, the conscience, the affections; it underlies all dispositions and habitudes, and is felt in all the thoughts and desires.   All moral qualities inhere in it as properties inhere in substance.   It is to the moral faculties of man what extension is to matter—the very form of their existence.

As natural life has its characteristic functions, so spiritual life has its distinguishing tendencies.   They all point to God. The very essence of a holy nature is sympathy with the Divine perfections—a state of the soul which harmonizes with the Divine will; which attracts it to God; which produces a communion, a fellowship, a familiarity, if I may so speak, that instinctively detects the impressions of God wherever they are found.   It is fundamentally the principle of LOVE to Him; its true expression is that of union with Him; and even where there is no direct reference to His name, it gives tone and complexion to all moral and intellectual exercises.   This love to God, not as a single habit, not as a series of particular affections, but as the ground-form of all, as the fundamental law of their manifestation, is the nearest approach we can make to the description of Holiness

as a state.   This is the reason why fellowship with God must
be the perfection of a holy being.   Love demands it.   Communion is the life of love ; and this, too, is the reason why
love is said to be the fulfilling of the law : not that benevolence or any individual sentiments of kindness, not even that
the adoration and praise of God's excellencies or gratitude
to Him as single and independent exercises, fulfil the law ;
but that state of the soul which is in deepest harmony with
God, and finds its full manifestation only in a sense of union
and correspondence with Him, contains the elements of all
true virtue.   Here is their centre of unity and their point
of divergence.   Schleiermacher was right in making the
essence of religion, subjectively considered, to be *feeling*, in
the extended sense which he has given to that term, but he
was wrong in making that feeling a sense of absolute dependence upon God.   Had he put love for dependence, and
distinguished between it as a pervading tone of the mind
and as manifested in special operations, his analysis would
have coincided substantially with that of the beloved Apostle : He that dwelleth in love dwelleth in God and God in
him.   So also there is a subjective unity in sin.   Depravity,
like Holiness, is a generic state—the law of a mode of existence and operation.   It is denominated in the Scriptures
death; and the term is happily chosen, as it impressively
exhibits its pervading influence upon all the powers and
faculties of the man.   The question of total depravity could
never have been raised if the Scripture notion of depravity
had been steadily apprehended.   It must either be total or
not at all.   The man who is dead is dead all over.   As the
ground-form of holiness is love to God, or rather the spirit
of love to God, so the ground-form of sin is the spirit of
opposition ; the carnal mind is enmity against God.

In this analysis of Holiness and Sin I maintain that the
Scriptures have rendered a real contribution to the philosophy of our nature.   The fact that there is an essential
unity in each had been previously felt and distinctly asserted
by the Peripatetics and the Stoics, but in what that unity

consists, their ignorance of God and of all true communion with Him precluded them from the possibility of answering. The unrenewed man is destitute of those elements of consciousness out of which alone an answer could be reflectively extracted. It was reserved for Christianity, in revealing the true God, to reveal, at the same time, the moral excellence of man. The scriptural account of Holiness resolves a difficulty which, I apprehend, every thinking man has felt, in explaining the effects which the history of the Fall attributes to a single sin upon a nature originally upright. If we were left to conjecture and speculation, we might suppose that, as a habit is not likely to be formed from a single act, the principle of rectitude would still remain, though weakened in its power, and by vigorous and systematic efforts might recover from the shock which, to some extent, had disordered the moral constitution. Bishop Butler[1] speaks with hesitation in relation to the degree of injury which might be expected to accrue from the first full overt act of irregularity, though he has no backwardness in regard to the natural results of a confirmed habit. The difficulty is created by overlooking the reality of government and the peculiarity of Holiness. In contemplating the effect of the first transgression on the part of an upright creature, we are not to confine our view to the tendency of the act to form a habit, as if the law of habit were the only law under which it does its mischief. We are to bear in mind that as we are under government, as well as possessed of a moral constitution, it has also judicial consequences which must enter into the estimate of the extent of injury sustained by the inner man. Now, as Holiness, which is the foundation of the virtuous principle—the keystone of the arch which maintains an upright nature in its integrity—consists essentially in union with God, whatever alienates Him must destroy it. This is precisely what every sin does; it provokes His curse, breaks the harmony of the soul with Him, and removes that which is the fundamental principle of all true excellence.

[1] Analogy, Part i., chap. 5.

The sinner must die; the moment that God frowns in anger death invades the soul. It is the judicial consequence of sin.

3. The third and last point to which I shall advert, as distinguishing the ethical teaching of the Bible, is the answer which it gives to the question, How shall man accomplish the end of his being? How shall he acquire that perfection of nature, that holiness of state, without which he can never see God and live? There is evidently a double work to be done—a change to be effected in his judicial relations, and in the temper and dispositions of the soul. As to the method of achieving the first, philosophy is completely dumb. The scheme of redemption, by which pardon and acceptance are secured, is necessitated by no principles of natural light; it is the offspring of infinite wisdom begotten by infinite grace. But philosophy may aspire to institute a discipline by which the sinner shall restore his shattered constitution to integrity, and attain the perfection to which he was originally destined. There is a strong feeling in us all that, though damaged, we are not ruined by the Fall, that we still possess the elements of our ancient greatness, and that by care and diligence on our part we can repair the mischief that has been done.

I am far, very far, from detracting from the benefits of a moral education, or saying aught to depreciate the importance of the most scrupulous self-culture. We can accomplish much by energy of purpose, by fidelity to conscience, by sensibility to honour. We can employ the principles of our nature, fallen though it be, in the consummation of a character which shall be distinguished by habits of nearly every specific virtue. The virgins who went up and down in quest of them might have gathered all the limbs of the mangled body of Osiris and put them together in their order, but it would not have been Osiris himself. We can form habits of nearly all that is materially right, and yet be wanting in the true principle of Holiness. It is a great mistake to suppose that *total depravity* means devilish wickedness. Death is one thing, and the putrefaction of the body another.

Now, the Scriptures teach us that the highest attainments of nature are only dead works.   Left to itself, without check or hindrance to its spontaneous developments, it would produce nothing but wicked works; but modified by education, by example, by society, and the thousand influences which co-operate in the formation of character, it may exhibit the loveliness of life on the features long after life has fled. Man can only act in obedience to his *nature ;* from the very definition of this term it is the law of his mode of existence or of life.   He can never, therefore, escape from the pervading power of depravity.   He may check one tendency by another and counteract one motive by another; just as in the physical world one law may be made to control another, and effects be produced by their combination which neither could singly produce.   But he can never rise above these laws; all his power, after all, is in obedience.   So man can never rise above his nature—all education is within its sphere.   Hence the utter and absolute impossibility of transferring himself from a state of depravity to that of holiness. He must be BORN again.   The new nature must be imparted, and as it tends to God, it must come from God.   Until the Divine Spirit shall renew us we are incompetent to perform a single work that is acceptable to God.   The victims which we bring to the altar are only lifeless carcasses.   It is idleness to talk of a discipline in Holiness to him to whom the *primum mobile* is wanting.   Neither does the Bible leave us, after imparting the elemental germ of Holiness, to the principle of habit or any other law of development and growth to effect the perfection of our being.   Having brought us into a state of fellowship with God, it maintains that fellowship by constant communications of His love, by unceasing assistances of grace.   We are committed to the tuition of the Holy Ghost, and under His guidance and inspiration we rise from one form to another until we are rendered meet for the inheritance of the saints in light.   Hence, the subjective states in which our Holiness is manifested are not denominated habits, but *graces.*   They are not acquisitions, but gifts; and to remind us perpetually of the source of all the excellence that attaches to us, the very language we employ is a confession of our own impotency and an acknowledgment of God's free favour.

I have now completed what I had to say upon the ethical system of the Bible. The true light in which redemption should be habitually contemplated is that of a Divine institute of Holiness. Its immediate end is to restore the union between ourselves and God which sin has broken. It starts out with the great thought that the Happiness of an intelligent and moral creature is not something foreign, not the possession of an outward and separate good, not shining courts nor splendid halls, nor any other princely equipage of state, but the exercise of its own energies in God. To be happy it must be in sympathy with the Author of its being. Upon this lofty eminence the whole scheme is erected, and all its arrangements are directed to the achievement of two results—the removal of those judicial consequences of sin which repel God from the sinner, and of those moral obstructions which repel the sinner from God. Jesus, as the Daysman betwixt them, comes in and lays His hand upon them both. He bears our sins in His own body on the tree, and thus reconciles God to us; He cleanses our hearts by the washing of regeneration, and thus reconciles us to God; and the first friendly interview of the parties takes place at the foot of the Cross when we believe in Jesus. This whole scheme involves the moral system—the system, if you please, of Divine philosophy— upon which the government of God is conducted. It is the ethical system of the universe, and the Gospel is the only means, accordingly, by which we can attain true integrity. In rejecting it we are not rejecting crowns and sceptres; we are rejecting the very essence of virtue, and it is idle to pretend to a profound reverence for rectitude when we disregard the only means by which we can be restored to it. In this moral aspect I am anxious to recommend it to you. All your present excellencies are dead works, and when the influences which now embalm and preserve the corpse are gone, it will putrefy and stink. The first step in real moral improvement is faith in the Son of God. When that step is taken we begin to live; until then we are dead in trespasses and sins.

DISCOURSE II.

THE LOVE OF TRUTH.

THE injunction of the Apostle, to think on whatsoever things are true, obviously implies that the love of truth for its own sake is a habit which we are bound to cultivate and cherish. If it is the circumstance of their being true which entitles these things to our attention and regard, and makes it our duty to investigate and pursue them, there must be something in truth, essentially considered, which commends it to the moral approbation of the species. It is to be regretted that philosophers, in commenting upon the obligation of veracity, have not paid sufficient attention to the habit or general disposition of the soul which lies at the foundation of every form of the virtue—of accuracy in narrative, sincerity in conduct, and fidelity to engagements. Commentators have even gone so far as to maintain that the Apostle in the words before us had his eye only upon that species of truth which relates to the social intercourse of men, taking it for granted that this is the only kind of truth to which an ethical character pertains. One[1] represents him as describing " moral characters and the duties of a Christian," and accordingly restricts his meaning to " integrity and uprightness in opposition to hypocrisy, insincerity or moral falsehood." The conviction seems to be common that the operations of the understand-

[1] Dr. Watts. Sermon on Phil. iv. 8.

ing are not immediately under the cognizance of conscience, and that of the processes by which we form our speculative opinions virtue and vice can neither be affirmed or denied. These speculations are often directed to subjects in their own nature indifferent, and it is confidently inferred that, because the objects of our thoughts have nothing to do with the distinctions of morality, our thoughts themselves are equally exempt from a moral character. Hence has arisen the dogma that we are not responsible for our opinions. The understanding is treated as a series of faculties, subject to its own laws, moving in a peculiar and restricted sphere, having no other connection with conscience than as it analyzes and applies the rules of morality to the cases of practice which are constantly occurring in the business of the world. It may study, arrange and digest the moral code, but the laws which it acknowledges have no reference to its own processes, but only to the conduct of life.

This, however, is not the doctrine of the Scriptures. They represent the domain of morality as extending to the whole nature of man. Whatever directly or indirectly falls under the jurisdiction of the will possesses an ethical character, and may be the occasion to us of praise or blame, according to the principles and habits by which we have been governed. The morality does not attach to the processes or faculties themselves, but to the spirit and temper, the motives and purposes, which have shaped and determined their operations. There is a general sense in which all the elements of our spiritual nature are in subjection to the will. The springs of action in our appetites, affections and desires, with which we are endowed, all act blindly; they simply impel, but they do not direct. They cannot regulate their own motions, they cannot prescribe the extent or circumstances of their gratification, or determine the relative value of the objects which elicit them. They rouse the will, and that must consult the conscience and the understanding as to the course to be pursued. Corresponding to all these

springs of action there are moral laws in obedience to which
the will must control them. These laws, ingrained into the
nature and invested with the supremacy which belongs to
them, are so many habits of virtue the complement of which
makes up integrity of character. In the springs of action
themselves there is nothing directly virtuous or vicious—
they are simply indifferent. It is when they have put the
man in the attitude of motion that responsibility begins,
and according to the principles upon which he treats them
he is entitled to praise or blame. These motive impulses
are adjusted to the whole nature of man. Some spring from
the body and operate at periodic intervals, such as hunger
and thirst, the appetite of sex and the desire of repose.
There is nothing virtuous or vicious in any of the naked
appetites, but virtue and vice may attach to the methods of
their gratification. There may be excess, as in gluttony and
drunkenness; food may be unlawfully procured, or may consist of materials prejudicial to the health of the system.
Other springs of action are directed to the mind, among
which one of the most prominent is curiosity, or the desire
of knowledge. In this, also, there is nothing directly moral,
but an ethical character ensues the very moment the will
pronounces upon the manner, the ends and the extent of its
gratification. When the question arises, How shall this
desire of knowledge be gratified? there are moral laws in
conformity with which the will is compelled to decide.
Other springs of action are directed to the nurture and cultivation of the finer affections of the heart, and like those
already enumerated are indifferent in themselves, though
the modes, and measure, and objects of their indulgence are
equally subject to the jurisdiction of the conscience. As,
then, there are principles of action designed to stimulate
every department of our nature, and as the method, end and
extent of their operation are to be determined by the moral
understanding, every department of man's nature is brought
under the cognizance of moral law, and he may be virtuous
or vicious on account of his opinions and sentiments as well

as on account of his conduct. The law in conformity with which we are bound to regulate the impulses of curiosity is the love of truth. This law, written upon the heart, incorporated into the nature, strengthened into a habit, constitutes the measure of the morality of intellect. It is not merely an accomplishment, an excellence, a beauty ; it is an indispensable duty to aim at truth in all the excursions of the understanding. It is as much a moral obligation to seek for it in our opinions as to express it in our words or to manifest it in our conduct. We are responsible for the opinions which we form, not merely as these opinions are connected with conduct, or are probably the offspring of corrupt affections, but on the ground that the love of truth, in the whole extent and variety of its import, is an imperative and indestructible duty. This is the uniform teaching of the Scriptures. This is implied in the exhortation to buy the truth and sell it not, to seek that wisdom which is only another name for it as for hidden treasures, and to prefer its merchandise to that of gold and silver. Jesus Christ commends Himself to our confidence and love on the ground of His being the truth ; promised the Holy Spirit as the Spirit of truth ; denounced the vengeance of God upon those who believed Him not when He had told them the truth ; and makes it the glory of the Father that He is the God of truth, and the shame and everlasting infamy of the prince of darkness that he is the Father of lies. The eulogies directly and indirectly bestowed in the Scriptures upon truth, knowledge, understanding, wisdom, have special reference, we freely concede, to that department of truth which is the immediate subject of Divine revelation, but they would be evidently pointless and meaningless if truth in general were not intrinsically a good, and a good of such a nature as to lay the understanding under a formal obligation to receive it.

It is, indeed, as the ancients well expressed it, the food of the soul—*pabulum animi*. There is a natural congruity betwixt it and the structure of the mind. The one corre-

sponds to the other as light to the eye and sounds to the ear.
The existence of such a desire as curiosity is a clear intimation that man was formed for intelligence as well as for
action; and the adjustment of his faculties to the objects by
which he is surrounded is a command from God to exercise
them according to the laws by which He has defined their
operation in the acquisition of knowledge.   Aristotle,[1] having
divided the rational faculties of man into speculative and
practical, proceeds to determine what is the best habit of
each.   The best habit of anything he denominates its virtue,
and very justly observes that the virtue of each object is
ascertained by its fitness for performing its peculiar functions.   These faculties evidently point to truth—the one
speculative, the other practical—as their appropriate func-
tion, and hence are a call of God through the essential constitution of the mind to seek for wisdom.   This doctrine
seems to me to be expressly and directly taught in a passage
of the Eudemian Ethics[2] which has been the occasion of not
a little perplexity to the commentators.   The Stagirite there
makes God the principle of motion in the human soul, and
treats the fundamental deliverances of consciousness as inspi-
rations of the Almighty, more certain than any deductions
of science or reason, and as the conditions upon which all
subsequent knowledge depends.   God has made us cognitive
beings.   He has impressed upon us necessary and indestructible laws of belief; and if there be any force in the argument from final causes, we are obliged to regard the pursuit of knowledge as a part of the law of our being.   It is
the end of the mind to know, as it is of the eye to see, the ear
to hear or the heart to feel.   Every man is as distinctly organ-
ized in reference to truth as in reference to any other purpose.

It deserves farther to be remarked that it is the prerogative
of truth alone to invigorate the mind.   The distinctions of
sophistry and error may impart acuteness, quicken sagacity
and stimulate readiness, but what is gained in sharpness is

---

[1] Nichom. Ethics.

[2] Lib. vii., c. 14, quoted in Hamilton's Reid, p. 773.

lost in expansion and solidity. The minuteness of vision which falls to the lot of whole tribes of insects is suited only to a narrow sphere and to diminutive objects. The eye, which can detect the latent animalcules which teem in the air, the water and the soil, is incompetent to embrace in its range the glories of heaven or the beauties of earth. The dexterity and readiness which defences of falsehood are suited to produce is not a free, generous, healthful activity, but a diseased condition of the system analogous to that induced by fever or poisonous and stimulating potions. But truth is a food which the soul digests ; it strengthens and consolidates the mind, and is in every view worthy of the high encomiums which the ancient sages were accustomed to lavish upon the pursuits of their favourite philosophy as the wealth of reason, the culture and medicine of the soul, the choicest gift of heaven.

There is another aspect in which the love of truth, as the pervading law of our speculative inquiries, may be satisfactorily exhibited. The moral and intellectual natures of man are so intimately connected, their mutual dependence so nicely adjusted, their action and reaction so perfect and complete, that confusion of understanding is always accompanied with corresponding lubricity of principle ; and he whose perceptions of truth are not remarkable for clearness and precision will most surely be distinguished by an equal obscurity in his conceptions of rectitude. The moral duties which we are required to perform may be contemplated as speculative principles whose truth must be submitted to the decision of reason, as well as authoritative laws of the conscience whose precepts we are bound to obey. There must be an exercise of the reflective understanding in eliminating the primary dicta of our moral nature, and in determining the occasions and circumstances which call for the application of particular rules. The regulation of our conduct is not dependent upon instinct. Aristotle, among the ancients, was unquestionably in advance of every age which preceded the introduction of Christianity, and is still in advance of many who call them-

selves Christians, in his clear and steady perception of the
indissoluble connection betwixt the cogitative and practical
departments of man's nature in reference to duty. He treats
it as a distinction betwixt virtue and science that the latter
is restricted to one portion of the soul, while the former embraces all the elements of our being. "There are three principles," he affirms in the Nichomachean Ethics, "which,
either single or combined, are the sovereign judges of truth
and conduct. These are sensation, intellect and appetite.
Of these three, mere sensation cannot alone be the foundation of any judgment respecting the conduct—that is, the
propriety of action—for wild beasts have perception by sense,
but are totally unacquainted with propriety. Affirming and
denying are the operations of intellect; desire and aversion
are those of appetite; and since moral virtue implies the
habit of just election, and election or preference resolves itself
into deliberation and appetite, every act of virtuous preference requires that there should be accuracy and truth in the
comparison, as well as correctness and propriety in the
desire." In conformity with this reasoning he subsequently
denominates the moral election or preference peculiar to
man "an impassioned intelligence or reflecting appetite."
Who is not reminded of Bishop Butler's "sentiment of the
understanding or perception of the heart?" The investigation of duty involving so obviously the exercise of judgment,
those philosophers are not to be rashly condemned who attribute the power of distinguishing betwixt right and wrong
to the same faculty of the mind which, it is confessed,
distinguishes betwixt truth and falsehood. They feel that
the mental processes are so nearly identical that they cannot
but regard it as an unnecessary multiplication of original
powers to have a peculiar understanding conversant only
about moral truth, while another understanding is admitted
to exist which deals in truth of every other kind. Our
faculties, which are only convenient names for the various
operations of a simple and indivisible substance, derive their
appellation, not from the specific differences of the objects

about which they are employed, but from their general nature. The discovery of truth, it is maintained, is as much an end to the moral inquirer who is seeking, under given circumstances, to determine his duty, as it is to the physical philosopher, whose investigations cannot be legitimately pushed beyond the province of existing phenomena. The same laws of evidence, the same original principles, the same elements of human belief, and the same process of patient analysis and patient induction, are, or ought to be, common to both, and can no more be discarded with impunity by the one than they can be by the other.

This reasoning is certainly plausible, though not conclusive. There is judgment in the decisions of the conscience, and the laws in conformity with which that faculty pronounces what Kant calls its *categorical imperative* become standards of evidence, the constitutive and regulative principles of operation in all that pertains to rectitude and duty. Mere speculation could never suggest to us the notions of right and wrong, of virtue or a crime; but the materials which conscience supplies become the subjects of philosophic contemplation, and are worked up in the laboratory of reflection into abstract principles, which must react upon the conscience. The moral opinions framed by the understanding from the phenomena of conscience will constitute our code of right, and in the application of this code to the countless contingencies and diversified occasions of life there is room for the influence of judgment in determining what principles to apply. There can, consequently, be no progress in virtue beyond the merest elements or primary dicta of our moral constitution without progress in intelligence. Knowledge is as essential to responsibility as conscience. Hence a variable or fluctuating standard of truth necessarily introduces a variable and fluctuating standard of morals; whatever system legitimates error legitimates crime; whatever blinds the understanding corrupts the heart. The moral nature, developed side by side with the intellectual, and in a large measure dependent upon it, is always involved in the same ruin.

Rude and barbarous nations are as much indebted to imbecility of reason, superinduced by neglect of cultivation, false
associations or ill-judged discipline, for their mistaken apprehensions of good and evil in the practical details of life,
as to depravity of taste or perversion of moral sensibility.
Their deeds of darkness are performed without compunctious
visitings of conscience, not because that messenger of God
slumbers in the breast, or is bribed by the sinner to hold its
peace, or prevaricates in regard to the fundamental distinctions of right and wrong, but because that light is extin-
guished, that soundness of judgment is wanting, without
which it is impossible to discriminate in the cases presented.
The moral habits can no more expand nor take root down-
wards and bear fruit upwards, while the understanding, the
true sun of the intellectual system, is veiled in darkness, than
the plants and herbage of nature can flourish in beauty and
luxuriance without the genial light of the day.   The sense
of obligation is always just in proportion to the enlargement
of the mind with liberal views of the relations of mankind ;
and although the knowledge of the right does not necessarily
secure its practice, it does secure what is always of vast
importance to society—remorse to the guilty and a homage
of respect·to the good.   He that acknowledges a legitimate
standard of moral obligation will find in his conscience a
check to those crimes which, through weakness, he is unable
to suppress—a restraint upon those passions which, through
frailty, cannot be subdued.   The transgressor who violates
rules of unquestioned authority which his own understanding has deduced from the phenomena of conscience will
assuredly drive tranquillity from his bosom and repose from
his couch.   He sins indeed, but without that moral hardi-
hood which attaches to those who, in their blindness and
ignorance, put light for darkness, and bitter for sweet.   *They*
are the most dangerous offenders who tamper with the principles of rectitude itself, who seek to escape the reproaches
of conscience by degrading the standard of moral obligation,
who pursue peace at the expense of truth, and extinguish

the light that they may not behold the calamity of their state. The abandoned condition of the Gentile world, which the Apostle graphically describes in the first chapter of the Epistle to the Romans, is ultimately traced to the vanity of their thoughts and the darkness of their minds; and those to whom the Gospel is hid have their minds blinded by the God of this world, lest the light of the glorious Gospel of Christ, who is the image of God, should shine into them and reveal the glory of the Lord, by the contemplation of which they might be transformed into the same image from glory to glory. There is hope of reformation as long as the principles remain uncorrupted; but when the light which is in us is converted into darkness, when lies are greedily embraced and errors deliberately justified, the climax of guilt has been reached, the ruin of the character is complete, and the perdition of the soul, without a stupendous miracle of grace, seems to be inevitable. Shame and remorse, the usual channels through which amendment is produced, are always the result of consciousness of wrong—an affection which is utterly inconsistent with that complete degradation of the mind into which thousands have been sunk, and in which error is neither lamented nor admitted.

From the intimate alliance which subsists betwixt the understanding and the conscience, speculative falsehood must be fatal to the integrity of morals. He who trifles with the constitution of his nature in those primary convictions which lie at the foundation of all knowledge and philosophy—and error must be ultimately traced to some transgression of their laws—is cherishing a temper which shall soon rise in rebellion against the authority of conscience, and extinguish the only light that can convict him of crime. From the obscurity and confusion which have been permitted to shroud the understanding may be anticipated a deeper gloom which is soon to settle on the heart. That the moral conduct of men is not always answerable to the looseness of their speculative principles, is not to be ascribed to any redeeming virtue in the principles themselves, but to the restraints of society, and the voice of nature which licentiousness has not yet been able to suppress. The *tendency* exists, though accidental hindrances have retarded its development. The denial of the reality of truth and evidence will be attended with a corresponding denial of rectitude and sin. These remarks, though they appear to me to be intuitively obvious, are felt to be necessary in order to rebuke the growing impression that speculative principles have no immediate influence in regulating conduct. We live in an age of sophists. A man may believe anything or nothing, and yet if his actions are consistent with the standard of public decency, his principles are not to be condemned, and he is not to be charged with wickedness on account of them. In the formation of his opinions he is exempt from the moral law; conscience takes cognizance of nothing but the life. As if there could be any real virtue where practice is not the result of principle! As if the opinion were not the soul, life and being of all that is praiseworthy or excellent in the conduct! There can be no morality without intelligence, and if there exists in the bosom of the Almighty an eternal standard of truth, from which the law of righteousness proceeds, in conformity with which the arrangements of Providence are conducted and the relations of things adjusted, and by which alone the harmony of the world can be effectually promoted, the first step towards communion with the Father of lights is to recognize that standard, and to have its rays reflected upon our own consciences. The mind cannot move in charity nor rest in Providence unless it turn upon the poles of truth. "The inquiry of truth," says Bacon,[1] "which is the love-making or wooing of it, the knowledge of truth which is the presence of it, and the belief of truth which is the enjoying of it, is the sovereign good of human nature. The first creature of God in the work of days was the light of sense, the last was the light of reason, and His Sabbath-work ever since is the illumination of His Spirit."

[1] Essay on Truth.

The last consideration which I shall adduce, in order to show the ethical character of the love of truth as the pervading law of intellectual speculations, is the circumstance that it is the general habit of mind of which honesty, frankness, sincerity and faithfulness are only specific manifestations. There is no method of argument by which the obligation of veracity, in the ordinary intercourse and business life, can be established which will not equally apply to the doctrine in question. Whatever evinces the wickedness and sin of voluntarily imposing upon others, will evince with equal certainty the wickedness and sin of voluntarily imposing upon ourselves. We have no more right to deceive ourselves than we have to deceive our neighbours. That state of the understanding in which it is exempt from prejudice, and judges according to the light of evidence, is only a different manifestation of that general condition of the soul in which it rejoices in rectitude, delights in sincerity, and scorns every approximation to concealment or hypocrisy. Few are sensible of the close alliance which subsists between partiality to error and duplicity and fraud in conduct. They are shoots from the same stock, fruits of the same tree. He that lies to his own understanding, or, what amounts to the same thing, does not deliberately propose to himself *truth* as the end of all his investigations, will not scruple at deceit with his neighbours. He that prevaricates in matters of opinion is not to be trusted in matters of interest. The love of truth is honesty of reason, as the love of virtue is honesty of heart; and so impossible is it to cultivate the moral affections at the expense of the understanding that they who receive not the truth in the love of it are threatened in the Scriptures with the most awful malediction that can befall a sinner in this sublunary state—an eclipse of the soul and a blight upon the heart, which are the certain forerunners of the second death. The spirit of leasing is always one. What, in regard to speculative opinions, we denominate sophistry, is a species of the same general habit which developed into action gives birth to the character of the knave, distinguished from the man of probity and wisdom, not more by the meanness of his views and the littleness of his ends than the number and minuteness of his contrivances to reconcile villainy with fair appearances. The sophist of speculation is the hypocrite of practice. The same temper which prompts us to prevaricate on one subject will prompt us to prevaricate on all. As the soul is one and indivisible, and understanding, affections, memory and will are only terms expressive of conditions in which the same substance is successively found, or forms of action which the same substance successively puts forth, whatever indicates disease in one mode of operation must, from the simplicity of its nature, affect it in all. As in music it is the same key which pervades the tune, whatever may be the variety of notes of which it is composed, so there is a general tone of mind which distinguishes all its activities, and gives harmony, consistency and unity to its various processes in every department of thought and feeling. There is a characteristic complexion, a pervading temper, which may be found alike in the tenor of its opinions, the trains of its reasoning and the sentiments of the heart. If that temper be the love of truth, the whole man will be distinguished by candour, sincerity, openness and generosity; if the spirit of leasing, the whole man will be distinguished by duplicity, treachery, equivocation and concealment. The love of truth is, accordingly, the great moral law in conformity with which curiosity must be regulated; it is the morality of the intellectual man, being to the understanding what sincerity is to the heart.

The only plausible objection which can be sustained against the conclusiveness of these views, which bring the understanding under the control of conscience and subject the motives to intellectual effort to the jurisdiction of morality, is that which assumes that the operations of the mind in the department of speculative truth are exempt from the authority of the will. Reid was unquestionably right in the enouncement which, so far as I know, he was the first distinctly and broadly to make, that virtue and vice are impossible where there is no exercise of the will. It has accordingly been contended by philosophers of no less note than Sir James Mackintosh, Lord Brougham, and the author of Essays on the Formation of Opinions, that as the assent of the understanding is always involuntary, being the necessary result of the evidence submitted to its view, no moral character can attach to our opinions. We cannot on account of them be either the subjects of praise or blame, of reward or punishment. By one, they tell us, who has mastered the successive links in a chain of mathematical reasoning the conclusion can no more be resisted than light can be excluded from the open eye. The design of these illustrious men in maintaining the innocence of opinion is worthy of all praise, but they have certainly confounded questions that are entirely distinct. Their purpose was to lay a broad basis for civil toleration and for mutual charity. They wished to transfer opinions from the jurisdiction of the magistrate, and to rebuke the clamours of bigotry, intolerance and sectarian zeal. For this purpose, however, it was not necessary to prove that man is not responsible for his opinions at all, but only that he is not responsible to his fellows. Persecution is not the offspring of the doctrine that responsibility attaches to opinion, but that this responsibility is directed to the magistrate. The Scriptures consequently put responsibility upon its proper ground when they show that though we are responsible, we are responsible only to God. We are not the masters of each other's faith. We are not at liberty to judge or despise our brother in consequence of his differences from us, but still each man must give account of himself to God. He may sin in his opinions, but we are not the persons to punish him for his guilt. To his own Master he stands or falls. These remarks are made in order to guard against the impression that in combating the argument for toleration we are opposed to the principle of toleration itself. On the contrary, it seems to us that the philosophers in question have left it in a much more precarious condition than they found it. But to pass this over, the same method of argument to which they have resorted in this case might be employed, with equal pertinency and force, to prove that there is no responsibility for the emotions, affections or permanent conditions of the heart. Love and hate are as much beyond the immediate province of the will as doubt or belief. These passions depend upon the presence or conception of qualities which just as necessarily excite them as evidence produces conviction. Even the determinations of the will itself are not exempt from the influence of the great law of causation, and if the argument is pushed to the extent of its legitimate application, conduct will' be as lawless as opinion. The connection betwixt motives and action is not less intimate and necessary than that between evidence and faith. It is precisely because there is this connection that responsibility in either case becomes conceivable or possible. If evidence had no inherent and essential tendency to generate belief, if conviction were the arbitrary offspring of circumstances, why should we be bound to examine evidence at all? and if motives had no inherent and essential tendency to terminate in conduct, why should we be bound to cultivate right affections? Let those who hope to escape from responsibility by resorting to metaphysical distinctions, beware that they are not entangled in their own net, and that in the issue they do not establish what they are trying to overthrow.

The fallacy, however, of this popular argument is easily detected. It consists in restricting the application of the will to the final determination to act—in making *will* synonymous with *volition*. But when morality is confined to the province of the will, that faculty is made to embrace all the wishes and desires, all the appetites and habits, which constitute the springs of human action. Morality prescribes to them their laws; and whenever these active principles are indulged in contravention of those laws, there guilt necessarily ensues; whenever in obedience to those precepts, there virtue and rectitude obtain. The sole question therefore is, whether vicious propensities and desires have any influence upon the operations of the mind—whether good or bad emotions can exert any sway in directing its efforts and giving shape to its results. The answer here is too obvious to be denied. The illustrations derived from mathematical demonstration are singularly unfortunate. The reasonings of necessary science are subject to none of those disturbing influences which, as we shall subsequently see, the mind experiences in practical inquiries from its tastes, its temper and its prejudices. There is in this case no coloured glass to tinge the light as it passes to the eye. Besides, the contradictory of a necessary truth is not only false but absurd, and to entertain it, or even to represent it in thought, is a simple impossibility. The will has no jurisdiction, because the subjects embraced are wholly beyond its province. This is implied in the very epithet by which this species of truth is signalized. It is very different with moral speculations. There, as every question has two sides, and the opposite of truth is always cogitable, the assent is not the product solely of the evidence, but of the evidence conjointly with the temper and disposition of the man. Two factors conspire in the production of the result. The mind not only receives the light, but changes and transforms it into its own image. The will, in its wide sense, enters as a powerful element, and puts its own interpretation upon the appearances submitted to the intellect. It does for the evidence what, according to the philosophy of Kant, the understanding does for the material of sensibility—it supplies the form. Hence, in moral and religious subjects universal experience has demonstrated that a man "understands as much by his affections as his reason." His beliefs are voluntary, in the sense that they are largely determined by the active princi‐ ples of his nature. Then, again, there is an indirect and mediate power of the will by which, although we cannot immediately produce any given conviction or emotion, we can place ourselves in the circumstances in which the causes shall operate that are fitted to achieve the desired result.

Upon these two grounds we maintain that there may be a virtuous or a vicious exercise of the understanding, and that man is responsible for his opinions as he is responsible for the motives which impel him to intellectual effort, and for the diligence, caution and attention by which he avails himself of all the means of arriving at truth.

I have designedly taken this wide circuit as preparatory to the illustrations, which are yet to be presented, "of the nature of that veracity which is incumbent on us in our intercourse with our fellow-creatures. The most solid foundation for the uniform and the scrupulous exercise of this virtue is to cherish the love of truth in general, and to impress the mind with a conviction of its important effects on our own happiness and on that of society." If asked why the love of truth is a duty, I can only appeal to the dictates of conscience and the authority of God. It is worthy of remark, however, that no theory of morals has ever yet been ventilated, at all entitled to the respect of mankind, in which this virtue has not received a prominent position. Among the ancients all virtue was a species of truth; and in the school of the Stagirite prudence was an intellectual habit conversant about all practical, as wisdom was a habit conversant about all speculative, truth. In the school of the Stoics the importance which is attached to it may be seen from the Offices of Tully. "Of all the properties and inclinations of men, there is none," he informs us, " more natural and peculiar to them than an earnest desire and search after truth;" and to this instinctive love of truth in general he traces our approbation of frankness, candour and sincerity in conduct. Among the Stoics, as among the Peripatetics, prudence as a cardinal virtue consisted in the contemplation and study of practical truth. The theory of Wollaston, to come down to modern times, confessedly resolves all virtue into truth; and the schemes of Clarke, Cudworth and Price presuppose the speculative conclusions of the intellect as the final basis of moral distinctions.

If we place virtue in sentiment, there is nothing, according to the confession of all mankind, more beautiful and lovely than truth, more ugly and hateful than a lie. If we place it in calculations of expediency, nothing on the one hand is more conspicuously useful than truth and the confidence it inspires; nothing, on the other, more disastrous than falsehood, treachery and distrust. If there be, then, a moral principle to which, in every form, humanity has given utterance, it is the obligation of veracity. Truth is alike the perfection of the intellect and the glory of the heart. The Gospel, it has been beautifully said, " divides universal virtue into two cardinal, collateral and co-existent branches —truth and charity, the foundation and consummation of all things, corresponding to the two constituent parts of human nature, the intellect and the will, those singular and supereminent distinctions by which man becomes the subject of a religion which makes him wise unto salvation."

The practical conclusion which I am anxious to impress upon you, from this part of the subject, is the obligation of making truth for its own sake the great end of your intellectual efforts. It is a principle which requires to be strengthened by exercise and matured into a habit. The discipline of the mind is imperfect, however fully its various capacities have been developed, until the love of truth gains the ascendency which is due to it as the supreme and sovereign law of thought. Various motives may prompt us to be diligent and patient in the acquisition of knowledge. Some seek it, as Butler has caustically suggested, merely for the sake of talking, or to qualify themselves for the world, some for their own entertainment, some for one purpose, others for another; but multitudes have no sort of curiosity to see *what is true*. There are subordinate ends which are lawful, but they must always be kept in subserviency to the love of truth for itself. What an influence it would exert upon all who are engaged in intellectual pursuits if they were pervaded in the whole soul with this pure and sacred love of knowledge! What student could indulge in indolence, or turn to his lessons as a weary task, or immerse himself in habits which dim the understanding, if he felt in any just proportion to the real state of the case the transcendent excellence of truth or the loathsome deformity of error? Let us rise to the dignity of this high argument. We have minds that were made to *know*—we are constructed with a reference to truth, and we are called upon to purge and unscale our sight at the fountain itself of heavenly radiance. The streams of science are flowing at our feet, and the food which angels eat is offered to our palate. Let it never be said that we have neglected these golden opportunities and turned from the temple of truth to worship at the shrine of ignorance, error and shame. Resolve in the strength of God this day that, like Isis in search of the mangled body of Osiris, you will go up and down gathering, limb by limb, the scattered fragments of truth as your circumstances shall enable you to find them.

This love of truth, which I have been endeavouring to recommend, will be of the very last importance to you to guard you against the deceits of the world. Man walketh in a vain show. Untutored by experience, the young, particularly, are slow to suspect that the prospects of good, of pleasure, opulence and power which stretch in rich luxuriance before them are an empty pageant. Unskilled in the treachery of the heart and the wiles of the tempter, they can hardly be persuaded that the gilded colours in which imagination adorns the future are only a splendid drapery under which are concealed disappointment, sorrow and vexation. They have yet to learn the emptiness of pleasure, the agonies of power and the vanity of wealth. Impetuous in their passions, ardent in their temper and ignorant of life, they are prone to fix their affections upon some of those beggarly elements which will crumble into ashes at the touch of experience. The Prince of Darkness, intent upon their ruin, plies his fatal arts of enchantment to lull them into a sleep of false security, to exclude religion from their thoughts, and to conduct them by deceitful promises of good, by lies congenial with his nature, to the shades of death. This is a position

of immense peril.   The world, the flesh and hell all conspire
by glozing falsehood to seduce us to perdition.   A covering
is spread upon the grave and the pit, and the ways of sin are
adorned with all that can please the eye, fascinate the ear or
enchant the heart.   Our security against these dangers is
conviction of the truth.   The Word of God, which is pre-
eminently the truth, and in which a truth-loving heart will
lead us to rest, dissipates the spell, reveals the snare and
delivers from the plot.   It paints life in its true colours,
tears the mask from the face of guilt, disrobes the world of
its gorgeous drapery and points to Him who is emphatically
the way, the truth and the life.   All the rays of moral truth
ultimately centre in the Cross of the Redeemer ; and we
never reach the summit of wisdom until we attain that life
which is alike the knowledge of the Father and of His Son
Jesus Christ.   Every one, says the Saviour, that is of the
truth heareth My voice.   None perish but those who love
darkness rather than light.   A deceived heart turns them
aside.

DISCOURSE III.

THE LOVE OF TRUTH.

IN my last discourse I endeavoured to demonstrate that the love of truth, as such, is a duty from the constitution of the human mind; the aptitude of truth to enlarge and expand it; the intimate connection betwixt the culture of our moral and intellectual powers; and the impossibility of vindicating the obligation of specific forms without recognizing the obligation of truth in general. I was led to show that we are responsible for our opinions in so far as we are responsible for the motives and influences under which we form them—that the operations of the understanding have a moral character, inasmuch as the impulse of curiosity, like all our other springs of action, is subject to the direction and control of the moral faculty. The love of truth for itself was evinced to be the law in conformity with which all our intellectual processes should be conducted. The end of every inquiry should be knowledge, the aim of every investigation simple and unadulterated truth. To guard against the possibility of misapprehension, it may be well to add that, in inculcating the love of truth as a moral obligation, it is by no means my purpose to imply that all men are bound to know all truth. There is a great difference betwixt asserting that nothing should be sought which is not the truth, and that everything which is the truth is the appropriate pursuit of every understanding.

There are departments of inquiry from which the natural limitation of our faculties precludes us; there are subjects upon which we are incompetent to speculate from the want of congruity betwixt them and the constitution of our own minds, and as long as our powers remain what they are they must for ever be to us an unknown world. All knowledge, as I have elsewhere demonstrated at some length,[1] is relative in its nature and phenomenal in its objects. Whoever, therefore, would seek to penetrate into properties of things to which our faculties are not adjusted, overlooks a fundamental condition of the possibility of knowledge, and his conclusions are entitled to no more respect than the speculations of a blind man upon colours or of a deaf man upon sounds. There are conditions in the objects corresponding to conditions in the subjects of knowledge; one thing is set over against another, and beyond the limits of this correspondence it is folly to push our inquiries. Omniscience is the prerogative of God alone. Men and angels, all creatures however exalted, must be for ever doomed to write over boundless regions of truth, " Hades, an unseen world." There is light there—light in which God dwells and rejoices—but which created eyes are not fitted to receive. To inculcate the obligation of universal knowledge is to tell men to forget that they are men, and to urge them upon attempting to be gods. It is to inculcate the most daring presumption, to sanctify intolerable arrogance and blasphemy. The duty to seek knowledge can never transcend our capacities. We are not bound to know what our faculties are unable to grasp, and the attempt to become wise beyond the laws of our nature has always been rebuked in the history of philosophy with the most signal and disastrous failures. Neither is it the duty of all men to seek all the knowledge which is attainable by any. The circumstances of multitudes are such that their inquiries are necessarily confined within narrow limits. Their time and attention

[1] See Second Review of Morell's Philosophy of Religion, in vol. iii. of this Collection.

are taken up with pressing cares, and the exigencies of life leave no leisure for abstracted speculation. The progress of knowledge, too, requires that those who are devoted to its interests should divide their labours. Some should be engaged in one department, some in another. Some should give themselves to the sciences, some to the arts, some to elegant letters, and others to the severer studies of logic, metaphysics and morals. In this way the march of humanity is accelerated, the general condition of society is improved, though no single individual can ever hope to be abreast of the whole culture of the age.

What particular department of speculative truth each man shall select for himself, and how far he shall prosecute his labours, are questions to be determined by the circumstances in which he finds himself placed. All that I assert in any case is that it is an indispensable duty in whatever inquiries we engage to aim only at the truth. We are not bound to endeavour after universal knowledge, but we are bound to guard against error and to receive nothing that has not the stamp of truth. All truth is not obligatory, but nothing but truth is obligatory, on the understanding. No man, under any circumstances, has a right to think a lie. He can no more without guilt administer poison to his understanding than he can administer it to his body.

The degree of knowledge which is essential to the discharge of the duties of any sphere in which a man is called to act, and to the accomplishment of his destiny as a moral and responsible being, is always binding. What the exigencies of our peculiar and distinctive vocations as artisans, labourers or members of the learned professions demand, and what our general calling, as men made in the image of God and destined to happiness or misery in a future state according to our character and conduct here, requires, it is incumbent upon all to seek, and it is possible for all to attain. That knowledge which pertains to the conduct of life is accessible to all upon whom the duties of life are imposed. It is the only knowledge which is of universal obligation, and in reference to it there is no need to inquire who shall ascend into heaven or who shall descend into the deep; the word is nigh us even in our hearts and our mouths. The great doctrines of man's duty and destiny are not left to doubtful disputations. They are proclaimed upon an evidence which is open, palpable, authoritative—they stand upon the testimony of God. Wherever the Scriptures are known it is the imperative duty of all to know Him, the only true God, and Jesus Christ whom He has sent. No cares, no business should be allowed to preclude us from the fountain of life; things temporal must yield to things eternal, things carnal must give way to the spiritual, the seen and perishing to the unseen and immortal. The Bible must have the precedence of every other book; and though a man could speak with the tongues of angels, and understand all mysteries and subdue all nations in obedience to his will, yet if he were destitute of that knowledge which makes him wise unto salvation, with all his boasted attainments he would be but a chattering fool, but as sounding brass or a tinkling cymbal. This knowledge, then, in its essential elements as bearing upon our destiny as men, is of universal obligation. This pearl of great price we must purchase though we sacrifice all our other possessions to gain it. With these explanations and limitations I proceed to point out in what the love of truth essentially consists, and to indicate some of the temptations to which the young particularly are exposed to disregard it.

I need not say a word in reference to the importance of these points. With all our commendations of the beauty, the glory, the excellency of truth, it must yet be acknowledged that the temper of mind which is most favourable to the successful pursuit of it is exceedingly rare, even among those whose professed business is to seek and explain it. Composed as men are of conflicting elements, as evidently disordered in their understandings as they are in their affections, liable to the perversions of passion and interest, apt to confound the zeal of prejudice with earnestness of principle, the affectation of vanity with brilliancy of genius, eager for applause, and not always scrupulous about the means of securing it, the last spectacle which they exhibit is the true spirit of philosophy, the motive which least vigorously impels them is the ingenuous love of knowledge. I cannot better introduce what I have to suggest upon the nature of the love of truth, which I have been endeavouring to commend, than in the words of Locke, a competent authority upon this subject, having been himself a distinguished example of the spirit he inculcates:

"First," says he,[1] "a man must not be in love with any opinion, or wish it to be true, till he knows it to be so, and then he will not need to wish it, for nothing that is false can deserve our good wishes, nor a desire that it should have the place and force of truth. Secondly, he must do that which he will find himself very averse to, as judging the thing unnecessary or himself incapable of doing it; he must try whether his principles be certainly true or not, and how far he may safely rely upon them. In these two things—viz., an equal indifferency for all truth: I mean the receiving it, the love of it as truth, but not loving it for any other reason before we know it to be true; and in the examination of our principles, and not receiving any for such, nor building on them, till we are fully convinced as rational creatures of their solidity, truth and certainty—consists that freedom of the understanding which is necessary to a rational creature, and without which it is not truly an understanding." We are not to confound the indifference of which Locke here speaks as to what is true previous to the discovery with indifference to the truth itself, neither are we to suppose that he commends a spirit which is at all indifferent to the search after truth. On the other hand, he would have us eager in the pursuit, impartial in our inquiries and established in our conclusions; zealous for truth, when truth is found, and ardent in quest of it while it yet lies undiscovered before us; guarding equally against the

[1] Conduct of the Understanding, sects. 11, 12.

partiality which would pervert and the lethargy which would
arrest the efforts of the understanding. He is a slave to
ignorance who is too idle to examine; he is a slave to prejudice who believes without, or independently of, evidence.
An exemption from indolence or apathy on the one hand, and
all irregular biases on the other—an exemption founded upon
the very anxiety to escape from the stagnation of ignorance
and the impostures of error—is the freedom of the understanding which Locke[1] pronounces to be essential to a
rational nature, without which it may be "conceit, fancy,
extravagance, anything," but not "an understanding." It
is this freedom which constitutes the love of truth, or rather
this freedom is the only means by which the love of truth
can be exemplified, and curiosity directed to its appropriate objects.

The whole duty of man in regard to the conduct of his
understanding may be referred to the single comprehensive
principle that evidence is the measure of assent. This is
the light which alone can make it manifest, and by this
light, and this light alone, are we commanded to walk. The
understanding, as the instrument of truth, has for its guide
the laws of belief, and it is in virtue of these laws that it is
so admirably adapted to the exercise of intelligence. Truth
to us is and can be only relative. Things in their own
natures, in their essences and quiddities, we are incapable
of apprehending. That alone is truth to us which the constitution of our nature either immediately or mediately
prompts us to believe. Its fundamental condition is confidence in our faculties, and the convictions which are produced in conformity to the laws of our rational nature, the
appearances of things to the human understanding when
healthfully exercised, these constitute the ultimate measures
of truth and falsehood. That *is* to us which *appears* to be,
and *is* only in so far as it *appears*. Beyond these *appearances* our faculties can never penetrate. Intelligence, or the
apprehension of truth, involves judgment, belief, conviction

[1] Conduct of the Understanding, sect. 12.

of certainty, not merely that the thing is there, but, to use a sensible analogy, *seen* to be there. There must be a constitution of mind adapted to that specific activity by which it believes and judges, as it is only by virtue of such a constitution that the conception of knowledge becomes possible. This preparation of the mind to know, or its adaptation to intelligence, consists in subjecting it to laws of belief under which it must conduct its own operations. Its energies can be exercised only under the condition that it *shall* know or believe. As it is the necessity of belief which distinguishes intelligent action from every other species of operation, there must exist in the mind, as a part of its very structure, natural tendencies to certain manners of belief, to be developed as soon as its activities are called forth. In their dormant state, as they exist antecedently to experience, they are only necessities of thinking; but developed by experience and generalized into abstract statements, they are original and elementary cognitions, the foundation and criteria of all knowledge. They are the standard of evidence, the constitutive and regulative principles of intelligence, the light of the mind; and without them the mind could no more be conceived to know than a blind man to see. Through them we know and believe everything else; they are vouchers and guarantees for all the truth which it falls to the lot of man to apprehend. To regulate belief by evidence is, accordingly, to receive nothing which is not either an original conviction or capable of being resolved into one. As we know by and through the mind, we can only know according to the laws of mind. All error may consequently be traced to some transgression of the laws of belief. There can be no doubt that, if all the conditions which ought to be observed in the processes of the understanding were faithfully regarded, there would be no danger of fallacy or mistake. Error is the result of disobedience or inattention to the intelligent constitution of our own nature, and the punishment of intellectual guilt. To follow nature, as that

nature came from the hands of God, is to be conducted to
truth as well as to duty.

If the primary data of consciousness are the standard and
measure of evidence, there are but two ways in which we
are liable to be misled and deceived. The first is, in assuming as an original conviction or the legitimate product of
such convictions, what is only the dictate of authority, custom, education or desire; and the second is, in misapplying
the data of consciousness to the cases which are actually submitted to the decisions of the understanding. We mistake
the real nature of the phenomena, and accordingly apply to
them laws which are not applicable. In other words, we
are liable to err by having a wrong standard of judgment
or by using a right standard improperly. These are the
heads to which it seems to me all prejudice, however origi-
nated, may be at last referred. They give rise to skepticism
and falsehood. He who confounds the dictates of education
or authority with the primary convictions of nature not
only exposes himself to the danger of serious and fatal mistakes, but prepares the way for the utter annihilation of the
essential distinctions betwixt truth and falsehood. The
origin and nature of skepticism have been admirably
described by Sir William Hamilton.[1] "Our knowledge,"
says he, "rests ultimately on certain facts of consciousness,
which, as primitive, and consequently incomprehensible, are
given less in the form of cognitions than of beliefs. But if
consciousness, in its last analysis—in other words, if our primary experience—be a faith, the reality of our knowledge
turns on the veracity of our generative beliefs. As ultimate,
the quality of these beliefs cannot be inferred; their truth,
however, is, in the first instance, to be presumed. As given
and possessed, they must stand good until refuted; *neganti
incumbit probatio*. Intelligence cannot gratuitously annihilate itself; nature is not to be assumed to work in vain, nor
the Author of nature to create only to deceive. But though
the truths of our instinctive faith must *originally* be admitted,

---

[1] Philosophical Discourses. Article on Brown.

their falsehood may subsequently be established; this, however, only through themselves, only on the ground of their
reciprocal contradiction. Is this contradiction proved? the
edifice of our knowledge is undermined; for no lie is of the
truth. Consciousness is to the philosopher what the Bible
is to the theologian. Both are professed revelations of Divine truth; both exclusively supply the constitutive elements
of knowledge and the regulative standard of its construction.
Each may be disproved, but disproved only by itself. If
one or other reveal facts which, as mutually repugnant, cannot but be false, the authenticity of that revelation is invali-
dated; and the criticism which signalizes this self-refutation
has, in either case, been able to convert assurance into scepticism—to turn the truth of God into a lie. As psychology
is only a developed consciousness, the positive philosopher
has thus a primary presumption in favour of the elements
out of which his system is constructed; while the sceptic or
negative philosopher must be content to argue back to the
falsehood of those elements from the impossibility which the
dogmatist may experience in combining them into the harmony of truth. For truth is one, and the end of philosophy
is the intuition of unity. Scepticism is not an original or
independent method. It is the correlevant and consequent
of dogmatism; and so far from being an enemy to truth, it
arises only from a false philosophy as its indication and its
cure. The sceptic must not himself *establish*, but, from the
dogmatist, accept his principles; and his conclusion is only
a reduction of philosophy to zero, on the hypothesis of the
doctrine from which his premises are borrowed. Are the
principles which a peculiar system involves convicted of contradiction, or are these principles proved repugnant to others
which, as facts of consciousness, every positive philosophy
must admit? then is established a relative scepticism, or conclusion that philosophy, so far as realized in this system, is
groundless. Again, are the principles which, as facts of consciousness, philosophy, in general, must comprehend, found
exclusive of each other?—there is established an absolute

scepticism; the impossibility of all philosophy is involved in the negation of the one criterion of truth. Our statement may be reduced to a dilemma. Either the facts of consciousness can be reconciled or they cannot. If they cannot, knowledge absolutely is impossible, and every system of philosophy therefore false. If they can, no system which supposes their inconsistency can pretend to truth." It is the office of the skeptic to bring the different powers of the soul into a state of unnatural collision and to set our faculties at war; to involve their functions in suspicion; to make the deductions of the understanding contradict original convictions of nature, or these original convictions contradict themselves in the conclusions they legitimate; and thus to sap the foundations of knowledge, to annihilate all certainty, to reduce truth and falsehood to a common insignificance, and expose the mind to endless perplexity, confusion and despair. The danger of receiving as maxims what are not entitled to the dignity extends much beyond the immediate errors in which they involve us. It is not that they generate a rash dogmatism, but that they afford the materials of undermining the whole temple of knowledge, which creates their mischief. The skeptic accepts them at the hands of the dogmatist and uses them as instruments of death. Hence, the importance, in the language of Locke,[1] of accustoming ourselves, "in any question proposed, to examine and find out upon what it bottoms. Most of the difficulties that come in our way, when well considered and traced, lead us to some proposition which, known to be true, clears the doubt and gives an easy solution of the question." The mischief which maxims rashly accepted as intuitive judgments or well-drawn conclusions have done to the cause of truth, both in philosophy and religion, is incalculable. A single crotchet of philosophers, that the relation of knowledge implies an analogy of the subject and the object, involved for centuries the whole subject of perception and the mode of our knowledge of the external world in confusion, hypothesis and contradiction.

[1] Conduct of the Understanding, Sect. 44.

The ideal theory was the offspring of this simple proposition; and·it might even yet retain its ascendency in the
schools, if the skepticism of Hume, at once the indication
and cure of the disorder, had not arisen and prepared the
way for a sounder metaphysics. The Scribes and Pharisees
took it to be a maxim that no good thing could come out of
Nazareth, and upon the absurd dogma founded the belief
that Jesus was an impostor. The " soft enthusiast " receives
it as an axiom that the benevolence of God rejoices in the
happiness of His creatures simply and for itself, and hence
proceeds to the denial of government, and especially the
operations of penal justice.

It deserves to be particularly remarked that the mind
very frequently assumes, without the formality of distinct
enunciation, as self-evident truths, a class of propositions
from which it would recoil if stated in words. It silently
and imperceptibly takes them for granted. They enter into
its reasonings without its being distinctly conscious of their
presence. Some men are tenacious of opinions because they
are the characteristics of a party or a sect—because they are
recommended by high authority, and have been sanctioned
by a long, uninquiring acquiescence. " When any of these
maxims are brought to the test" no man who pretends to
reason will hesitate to condemn them as fallible and uncer-
tain, and " such," as Mr. Locke expresses it,[1] " as he will
not allow in those that differ from him; and yet after he is
convinced of this, you shall see him go on in the use of
them, and the very next occasion that offers argue again
upon the same grounds."

The criteria by which the fundamental data of consciousness are recognized are sufficiently plain for all the purposes
of life. The difficulty consists not in their obscurity or
confusion, but in our own reluctance to examine the grounds
of our belief, and to bring every proposition to the law and
to the testimony. We love opinions instead of truth. We
are pleased with dogmas upon other and independent

[1] Conduct of the Understanding, Sect. 6.

grounds, and are insensibly led by our passions and desires to transform ourselves from candid and impartial inquirers into earnest and interested advocates. Education makes authority tantamount to nature, and we quietly treat as intuitively obvious what we caught from the nursery and cradle, without having ever seriously asked ourselves whether these principles are indeed distinguished by the marks and characters of original convictions. Hence, error is perpetuated from age to age. One generation transmits a legacy of lies to another, and the dreams of tranquillity are not disturbed until some threatening form of skepticism arises that compels examination and enforces inquiry. The first duty, therefore, which the love of truth exacts at our hands is to look well to our principles, to prove all things and to hold fast that which is good. Bring everything to the standard of evidence which our nature supplies. This is the only light which we are at liberty to follow. A blind and implicit reception of any principles, however sacred, without satisfactory evidence, is alike condemned by the Scriptures and the voice of reason. This mechanical faith is not an exercise of the understanding; it is a passive acquiescence in the circumstances which surround us. Such a man does not think, he is thought for; he simply crams himself with the cogitations of other minds, as a cook crams a bird with food. Let a man be rigidly indifferent as to what shall prove to be truth, keep all passion, interest or disturbing influences at a distance, and patient examination will most certainly conduct him to the light of real evidence.

The other form in which prejudice operates is by distorting the appearances of things, so as to make us upon true principles pronounce wrong judgments. Our faculties are not put in complete possession of the case. This is especially true of moral and religious subjects. In all such subjects the evidence is tinged by the complexion of the mind, and although the judgment may be right according to the evidence as presented, it is not right according to the evidence as it exists in itself. It is a jaundiced eye misjudging of colours. That there is a connection betwixt the state of the soul and the perception of moral and Divine truth was a principle admitted even by the heathen philosophers. Aristotle expressly enounces it, and the celebrated fable of the wolf learning to read was especially designed to illustrate it. Depravity of heart and the indulgence of corrupt and wicked passions not only give rise to false measures of truth, but false applications of the true measures of good and evil. In this double operation consists what the Scriptures denominate the deceitfulness of sin. Things are represented in disguise, bitter put for sweet, sweet for bitter, and through the " fatal force and imposture of words" the fraud is concealed and propagated. Thus, parsimony may have the credit of frugality, and a spirit of revenge be dignified as sensibility to honour, and extravagance or prodigality receive the praise which is due to liberality. The passions make out a false case, and hence a false judgment is necessarily rendered. The ablest advocate of the passions on such occasions is the power of association. Let unpleasant ideas be connected with a name, and they will be transferred to everything to which the name is applied. A "slaveholder" at the North is the very embodiment of evil, and an "abolitionist" at the South an emissary of darkness. It is the trick of politicians to bandy epithets, words being the "counters of wise men, but the coin of fools." You might not be able to injure a man's principles, but call him some hateful name and you effectually destroy him. There is no subject in regard to which the young should be more constantly on their guard than the sophistry of the heart. In a right-ordered mind adaptation to its state is the highest evidence of good, and when the heart is corrupt the things which are suitable to it will still be prized as objects of desire, and invested with all those properties and attributes which belong to real excellence. It will still make analogy or correspondence to its prevailing tastes and inclinations the practical criterion of truth. As the relation of assent can never freely and cheer-

fully obtain where the mind and proposition are not homo-
geneous—sympathy being in this, as in all other cases,
essential to union—it is clear that wickedness has a fearful
power in seducing the understanding into error. It has but
to seize upon this principle of fitness to make the feeling
of proportion to its own tastes, of correspondence and congruity with its own dispositions or desires the measure of
good, in order to fill the mind with prejudices, and to erect
a standard of practical truth which must fatally pervert the
judgment. Taylor has well observed that "a man's mind
must be like your proposition before it can be entertained,
for whatever you put into a man it will smell of the vessel.
It is a man's mind that gives the emphasis, and makes your
argument to prevail." Hence, as the same eloquent writer
again remarks, "It is not the wit of man, but the spirit of
a man, not so much his head as his heart, that learns the
Divine philosophy." Moral is not more distinguished from
mathematical reasoning by the fact that it admits of degrees
than by the equally important fact that these degrees may
be indefinitely modified by our tempers, dispositions and
habits. Even the transient humour in which we may
chance to be has often a controlling influence. The same
circumstance which in one state of mind would carry no
weight with it, in another might amount to a very high
degree of certainty, just as in one state of mind a phenomenon may be eminently suggestive which in another would
pass unheeded. Newton, no doubt, had often seen apples
fall, but the event was insignificant until he happened to be
in a particular vein of speculation. "Trifles," which to
the generous and unsuspecting seem "light as air, are to
the jealous, confirmation strong as proof of Holy Writ."
While, therefore, it is true that a man's faith will always
be according to his apprehension of the evidence, it is not
true that in moral subjects the evidence will always be
apprehended in its just proportions. It may be perverted,
distorted, discoloured or reduced to nothing; the facts which
contain it may fail to suggest it, or suggest it feebly and

inadequately. To a man under the habitual dominion of
covetousness it is impossible to represent in its true light an
enterprise of charity ; to a glutton lost in sensuality or a
sot reduced to the condition of a brute all discourses upon
man's sublime gifts must be unmeaning. The voluptuary
and debauchee cannot comprehend the dignity and excellence of self-denial. The proud will turn in disgust from
lessons of humility, and the envious sneer at the obligation
of benevolence. It is an universal rule that sin darkens
the understanding, while it corrupts the heart. It is as
inconsistent with the just appreciation of evidence as with
the faithful discharge of duty. Hence, it was a custom in
the ancient schools of philosophy to spend some time in
trials and examinations of the genius and disposition of
their scholars before they admitted them to the sublime
instructions of the sect. The Platonists, particularly, laid
down severe rules for " the purgation of the soul, for refin-
ing and purifying it from the contagion of the body, and the
infection it might have contracted from the sensitive life, in
order to fit and prepare it for the contemplation of intellectual and abstract truths." One greater than Plato or Aristotle, the Master of a nobler philosophy than ever sprang
from earth, has enjoined it as the condition of knowing
Divine truth that we cultivate the spirit of universal obedience. He that will do God's will shall know of the
doctrine.

There is no principle which needs to be more strenuously
inculcated than that evidence alone should be the measure
of assent. In reference to this principle the whole discipline of the understanding must be conducted. Our anxiety should be to guard against all the influences which
preclude the access of evidence, incapacitate us to appreciate its value, and give false measures of judgment instead
of the natural and legitimate laws of belief. All real evidence we are bound to receive according to the weight
which it would have in a sound and healthful condition of
the soul. It is a defect in the mind not to be able to appre-

ciate its lowest degrees. That is a feeble and must be a fickle mind which, foolishly demanding certainty on all the questions submitted to its judgment, cannot proportion its faith to the amount of light it enjoys. Dissatisfied with probability, and ever in quest of what the circumstances of our case put hopelessly beyond our reach, such men, like Noah's dove, will seek in vain for a spot on which they can rest. Probability is the guide of life, and he who resolves to believe nothing but what he can demonstrate acts in open defiance of the condition of sublunary existence. There are many things here which we can only see through a glass darkly. Our duty is to walk by the light which we have. God commands us to yield to all evidence that is real in precise proportion to its strength. Evidence, and that alone, He has made it obligatory on our understandings to pursue, and whatever opinions we hold that are not the offspring of evidence—that have come to us merely from education, authority, custom or passion—however true and valuable they may be in themselves, are not held by us in the spirit of truth. These measures of assent are only presumptions which should stimulate inquiry and breed modesty and caution. They are helps to our faith, but should never be made the props of it.

Hence, all efforts to restrict freedom of debate and the liberty of the press should be watched with caution, as prejudicial to the eliciting of evidence and the defence and propagation of the truth. But little is gained if opinions are crammed into men; and this is likely to be the case where they are not permitted to inquire and to doubt. At the same time it must be remembered that no spirit is more unfriendly to that indifference of mind so essential to freedom of inquiry than that which arises in the conduct of controversy. When we become advocates we lay aside the garb of philosophers. The desire of victory is often stronger than the love of truth; and pride, jealousy, ambition and envy, identifying ourselves with our opinions, will lend their aid to pervert our judgments and to seduce us from our candour. A disputatious spirit is always the mark of a little mind. The cynic may growl, but he can never aspire to dignity of character. There are undoubtedly occasions when we must contend earnestly for the truth; but when we buckle on the panoply of controversy, we should look well to our own hearts, that no motives animate us but the love of truth and zeal for the highest interests of man.

I am apt to suspect that the habit which is not unfrequently recommended, as a means of intellectual discipline, of arguing on the wrong side of a question as a trial of ingenuity and skill, is inconsistent with ingenuousness of mind. It is sporting with falsehood, trifling with evidence, and must eventually produce a fondness for sophistry, which will ultimately destroy solidity of judgment. Besides this, to use arguments as conclusive which we do not believe to be possessed of that character is very near to a deliberate lie. It is a practice closely allied to pious frauds.

But the most serious dangers to which a young man is exposed of surrendering the interests of truth are those which arise from vanity or shame.

The love of applause, which, studious only of appearances, substitutes hypocrisy for virtue, rashness for courage and pedantry for learning, will court reputation rather from the glitter of paradox than the steady light of truth. He whose end is to elicit admiration, who aims to *seem*, not to *be*, a philosopher, will prefer plausibility to evidence, ingenuity to reasoning and singularity to general consent. When the ambition of notoriety, which ought not to occupy the subordinate position of an incidental motive, usurps the place of an *end* of inquiry, its disturbing influences upon the integrity of the mind are not less disastrous than the effects of ostentation in morals upon the sincerity of the heart. The laws of evidence cease to be regarded; novelty, not truth, becomes the measure of assent; astonishment, not conviction, the aim of argument; and the stare of wonder is deemed a more pleasing tribute than substantial esteem. The excursions of this insane principle are marked by opposition to the settled opinions of the race fierce and malignant in proportion to their worth, and by a prolific ingenuity in the invention of error. As the reputation of sagacity and superior discernment is the prize to be won, he promises to be the most successful competitor who triumphs over the general persuasion of mankind, who detects flaws and elements of falsehood in the faith of generations, and rears a new fabric of wisdom and knowledge upon the ruins of ancient ignorance and superstition. To such men nothing is venerable, nothing sacred. They penetrate the depths of the past to collect the mischievous opinions which time had consigned to oblivion, and to reproduce upon the stage in the dress of novelty the actors that once inspired consternation and alarm. They explore the mysteries of science, not to admire the wisdom or adore the goodness of God; not to enlarge the dominion of mankind, to relieve their wants, to increase their comforts, to stimulate their piety and exalt their destiny; but to wring from the secrets of nature, by hateful processes of torture, some dubious confessions that may signalize themselves as unexpected ministers of ill. As religion is the most awful subject that can occupy the thoughts of men, it is here that the encroachments of vanity will be most daring and presumptuous. Science is the possession of but few, and he who ventures upon novelties in any of its departments can expect but a limited glory. Religion, on the other hand, is the property of the race, and he who should succeed in confounding its principles or extinguishing its sanctions would achieve a conquest which, if the extent of ruin is to be the measure of renown, might satisfy the largest ambition. It is a marvellous phenomenon that men should be willing to relieve obscurity by infamy— that rather than not be known, they will deliberately suppress the light of reason, quell the remonstrances of conscience, forfeit the approbation of the wise and good, defy the Omnipotent to arms and run the risk of everlasting damnation. Yet such there are, infatuated men, who seek for distinction in unnatural efforts to degrade their species—

who found a title to respect upon discoveries which link them in destiny to the brutes—who glory in their shame. Nothing in the majesty of virtue rebukes them, nothing in the simplicity of truth allures them, nothing in the terrors of the Almighty alarms them. With ruthless violence and parricidal zeal they attack whatever is venerable, sacred, august and true. The sublimest doctrines of religion, the dread retributions of eternity, and the name and perfections of Him who sits upon the circle of the earth and before whom the inhabitants thereof are as grasshoppers and the nations are counted as the small dust of the balance, are treated as materials to minister to vanity. At one time, under the pretext of exalting natural religion, the mysteries of the Cross are disregarded, and reason is professedly exalted only that grace may be really despised. At another time the distinctions of truth and falsehood are involved in confusion, and universal skepticism made the touchstone of sound philosophy; and truth, and duty, and religion disappear in the darkness. The scene changes, and we behold open apologists for Atheism, who seek to gain a name in the earth by unblushingly proclaiming that they can detect no traces of wisdom in the fabric of the world, no tokens of goodness in the conduct of Providence—whose deity is chance, whose devotion is sensuality, whose hope is extinction. But as these gross forms of impiety and absurdity soon excited too much disgust to flatter the vanity of their authors—the infamous odour they emitted rebuking the inspection of curiosity—this miserable ambition of distinction was compelled to resort to decency, and assuming the air of profound speculation, covered its enormities under the refinements of a philosophy in which names that are dear to the heart—the names of God, of virtue and religion—are retained, but the things themselves are exploded. This system is exactly adapted to the ruling passion of the vain. Obscurity is its element, and as objects look larger in a mist, the reputation of profound sagacity and wisdom may be cheaply purchased by substituting mystery for sense and dreams for thought, by drinking inspiration from the clouds, and clothing oracular responses in a jargon as dark and unintelligible as the hieroglyphics of those great exemplars of imposture, the priesthood of Egypt. Guard against vanity. Never let it be a question whether this or that opinion shall attract attention to your persons. Look only for evidence; follow the light; and be content with the reflection that you have deserved, whether you have gained or not, the approbation of your fellows. Wisdom will eventually be justified of all her children. The triumphs of vanity are short, those of truth everlasting.

Closely connected with vanity is the irregular influence of the sense of shame in prompting us to shrink from opinions which may expose us to ridicule. False shame, it is obvious, however, is not so fatal to the interests of truth as vanity, since, content with suppressing unpopular convictions, it makes no excursions into the fields of error. Unambitious of attracting observation, it meditates no monument of glory. It is not obscurity, but contempt, that excites its apprehensions. The sense of shame as a subsidiary sanction of virtue and propriety is an important, perhaps an indispensable, element in the economy of human nature. It is a protection from what is little in principle and mean in conduct. But to exalt the sense of the ridiculous into a criterion of truth, to make it the guide of reason in the pursuits of philosophy, is to destroy the just subordination of impulses and passions to the dictates of the understanding. Our emotions depend not upon the essential qualities of the objects that excite them, but upon the representations that are made to the mind. The eye affects the heart; the aspects or lights in which things are contemplated determine the character of the feelings they produce. If, then, virtue and truth are capable of being distorted by the fancy and presented under false appearances, they are capable of being made the occasions of emotions foreign to their nature. It may, indeed, be conceded that the sense of ridicule is an instinct of nature, and that its appropriate qualities are neither truth, virtue, nor goodness, distinctively as such; but as instances of virtue can be misrepresented to the moral sense and receive the censure which is due to vice, so truth can be covered in the disguise of falsehood, and provoke the laughter which is due to folly. The intrinsic dignity and importance of an object are no exemption from the shafts of raillery. The noblest painting may be seen in a false light. The history of infidelity is fraught with melancholy proof that no subjects are too sublime for levity, too sacred for caricature or too solemn for a jest. Could religion always be presented in its true colours—and this is the truth which it is most important to guard—it would have nothing to fear from the power of ridicule. But when piety is denounced as superstition, humility reproached as meanness, faith derided as enthusiasm, firmness despised as obstinacy, and joy in the Holy Ghost insulted as the offspring of spiritual pride, religion may suffer from the contempt due only to the gross and disgusting pictures which sophists and buffoons have drawn of it. There are a thousand tricks by which wit and humour may pervert the mysteries of the Cross, and connect them with low and ridiculous associations with which they have no natural affinity. Through the "fatal imposture of words," by mean and vulgar analogies, the eccentricities of good men may be artfully exaggerated, their ignorance and frailties conspicuously set off, and true piety dexterously confounded with hypocrisy and fraud. In every age skeptics have relied more upon the power of sarcasm than upon the power of argument. The enemies of Christianity, as Dr. Paley justly remarks, have pursued her with poisoned weapons. A sophism may be detected, but who can refute a sneer? When infidelity ceased to be confined to the circles of philosophers and began to court the approbation of the crowd, it abandoned whatever dignity and elegance it formerly possessed, and descended to the lowest forms of buffoonery. It dropped the mask of the sage, assumed the character of the harlequin, relinquished argument and betook itself to ribaldry.

The design of the French philosophers was not to discuss the merits of Christianity, but to present it in false lights, to exhibit it in uncouth and revolting attitudes, to attach disgusting or ridiculous associations with its peculiar doctrines, and to cover it with the contempt which was due only to the odious pictures themselves had drawn. It has been the trick of the profane in every age to deride pretensions to spiritual religion, and it requires no ordinary degree of courage to resist the contempt to which the profession of vital religion is exposed in the world. When it is industriously connected with ideas of littleness, meanness and fanaticism, represented as the property of narrow spirits and of coward hearts, the temptation is very strong to be ashamed of its doctrines, its promises and its hopes. Such is the depravity of men that singular virtue is made the object of reproach, while singular vice or singular error may be the means of distinction. Hence, our Saviour brings the awful sanctions of eternity to bear upon those who are in danger of surrendering truth to a jest, their honest opinions to raillery and banter. He points to a shame with which sin shall be finally accompanied, more tremendous and appalling than all the reproaches of men, an everlasting contempt which shall astonish and overwhelm the guilty, when God shall laugh at his calamity and mock when his fear cometh. " Whosoever is ashamed of Me, and of My words, of him also shall the Son of man be ashamed when He comes in the glory of the Father with the holy angels."

We should particularly guard against the irregular influence of shame, because its operations do not always stop at the suppression or concealment of obnoxious opinions. The rebukes of conscience must be silenced by pleas and the self-respect we have forfeited must be regained by evasions. He who is ashamed of the truth will soon proceed to condemn it. He who is afraid to profess Christ will soon be tempted to deny Him. He that is not prepared to suffer will soon be induced to betray. That character alone is great in which the love of truth is supreme, habitually superior to the clamours of prejudice, the surmises of ignorance and the jeers of contempt.

I have now described briefly and rapidly the characteristics of the love of truth, which was previously evinced to be a duty, and pointed out some of the dangers to which we are exposed of foregoing its claims. My design has been to commend this spirit to your hearts. It is the foundation of all solid excellence. It gives stability to character and distinguishes firmness from obstinacy. It makes the man of principle. You may be distinguished in the world without it, but you never can have the approbation of your own hearts or the smile of God. You never can perfect and adorn your natures. Learn to investigate, to examine, to try the principles that are proposed to you, and make it a fixed rule to regulate your assent by no authority but that of evidence. Never be in love with opinions upon any foreign or adventitious grounds; cleave to them only because they are the Truth. Hear instruction, and be wise, and refuse it not. "Blessed," says Divine Wisdom, "is the man that heareth Me, watching daily at My gates, waiting at the posts of My doors. For whoso findeth Me findeth life, and shall obtain favour of the Lord. But he that sinneth against Me wrongeth his own soul: all they that hate Me love death."

DISCOURSE IV.

SINCERITY.

TRUTH may be considered in two leading aspects, either as having reference to the correspondence of our convictions with the reality of things, which may be called *speculative* truth or truth of opinion, or as having reference to the correspondence of our expressions with the reality of our convictions, which in contradistinction from the former may be called *practical* truth or truth of life and conduct. The one protects our minds from imposition and error, the other protects our lips from treachery and falsehood. The one keeps us from being deceived, the other from deceiving. The love of truth, as a general habit, equally includes them both; it makes us cautious, discriminating and attentive to evidence in the process by which our opinions are formed, and exact, prudent and scrupulous in the testimony by which we communicate our judgments to others. The love of truth, as a general habit, and as applying to our speculative inquiries, has already been sufficiently considered. It remains now to discuss the second great branch of the subject—practical truth, or truth of life and conduct.

This seems to me to include three things. The first is *sincerity*, which obtains whenever the signs, whatever they may be, by which we intentionally communicate ideas, exactly represent the state of our own convictions. The standard of this species of truth is a man's own thoughts. As the design of speech is not directly and immediately to express the nature and properties of things, but our own conceptions in regard to them, he that utters his thoughts is not wanting in veracity, however those thoughts may fail to correspond to the realities themselves. Distinguished casuists have, accordingly, defined veracity to be a moral virtue, inclining men to represent phenomena according to their own apprehensions.[1] The matter of it they make twofold, immediate and remote;[2] the immediate consisting in the correspondence of the statement with the conviction of the speaker, the remote in the correspondence of the conviction to the thing itself. The concurrence of the two is a safeguard against all deception from testimony. It is then perfect and complete. With this double distinction of the matter of veracity, it is easily conceivable that a man may veraciously utter what is false and falsely utter what is true. If he affirms that to be true which he believes to be false, or affirms that to be false which he believes to be true, though

[1] Thomas Aquinas, Summa, 2. 2. Quest. 110, art. 1. Dens, Theol., Mor. and Dog., vol. iv., p. 306. De Veritate.

[2] The distinction of Aquinas is into matter and form—the matter of a proposition being its truth or falsehood abstractly considered; the form, its truth or falsehood according to the belief of the speaker.

A proposition may obviously be contemplated in two lights—either abstractly as a naked affirmation or denial, and then the matter of it is the thing, whatever it may be, which is asserted or denied; or relatively, according to the purpose and intention of the speaker, and then the matter of it is the apprehension of his own mind; it affirms or denies, not what is, except *per accidens*, but what he believes. When the question is in reference to the truth of the thing, the matter, in the first aspect, is the point of inquiry; when the question is in reference to the sincerity of the speaker, the matter, in the second, is all that is important. This is, indeed, the sole matter of veracity, but not the sole matter of the proposition. Hence, the distinction into proximate and remote is a convenient one, if it be borne in mind that the proximate is the essence of veracity as it respects the speaker; the remote, of the proposition abstractly considered as true or false. The most common distinction, however, is into matter and form; the matter having reference to the proposition itself—the form to the belief of the speaker.

in each case his belief may be erroneous and things be exactly as he represents them, he is guilty of deceit—he has spoken against his mind; the proximate or immediate matter of veracity is wanting. This proximate matter is what modern writers have denominated physical or logical, and the remote what they have denominated moral, truth. It is evident that in the former the essence of sincerity consists, and upon the latter the value of testimony, as an independent source of knowledge, depends. "If there be an agreement," says South,[1] who, in his definition of a lie, has followed Augustin—"if there be an agreement between our words and our thoughts, we do not speak falsely, though it sometimes so falls out that our words agree not with the things themselves; upon which account though in so speaking we offend indeed against truth, yet we offend not properly by falsehood, which is a speaking against our thoughts, but by rashness, which is affirming or denying, before we have sufficiently informed ourselves of the real and true estate of those things whereof we affirm or deny." It is certainly incumbent upon men to guard against imposture and error; and where their judgments have been hastily formed, without due attention to the evidence within their reach, or under the influence of prejudice and passion, their mistakes are not without guilt. They sin against the truth in the absence of that spirit of indifference, impartiality and candid inquiry in which the love of it consists, though they are not chargeable with insincerity or deceit in their communications to others. The difference betwixt a mistake and a lie is, that in the one case the speaker himself is deceived, in the other, he proposes to deceive others. A mistake always, a lie never, has the proximate matter of veracity.

The second branch of practical truth requires that our actions correspond with our professions. This is called *faithfulness*, and consists in fulfilling the engagements and meeting the expectations which we have knowingly and voluntarily excited. This subject is being discussed under

---

[1] Sermon on Falsehood, Prov. xii. 22.

the head of veracity; but faithfulness is evidently a mixed virtue, combining the elements of justice and of truth. A promise or a contract creates a right in another party; and the obligation to fulfil it arises, accordingly, not simply from the general obligation of veracity, but from the specific obligation which corresponds to my neighbour's right. Hence, breach of promise is something more than a lie; it is a fraud —it cheats a man of his own.

The third thing involved in practical truth is *consistency*, or harmony of character. Truth is one, and the life of the good man must be a reflection of its unity. Fluctuations and fickleness of opinion or of conduct are certain indications of gross dishonesty of heart, or of gross imbecility of understanding. When a man often shifts his principles, it is not truth, but imagined interest, that he stands on; and he who is under the frequent necessity, as the phrase goes, of "*defining his position*," has no position that is worth defining, and is fit for no position of any moment.

These three—sincerity, faithfulness and consistency—comprise the whole duty of practical veracity. The opposite of the first is *deceit* in its Protean shapes of lying, hypocrisy and flattery; the opposite of the second is *fraud;* and the opposite of the third is *inconstancy* or fickleness.

Before proceeding to a more detailed discussion of these subjects, it may be well to adjust a preliminary question in reference to the grounds of the obligation of veracity. Paley resolves them into contract.[1] "A lie," says he, "is a breach of promise; for whoever seriously addresses his discourse to another tacitly promises to speak the truth, because he knows that the truth is expected." To say nothing of the fact that a promise presupposes the veracity of the promiser as the measure of its engagement—that it is nothing and can be nothing except on the supposition that the promiser really conveys the purpose of his mind—the theory labours under another difficulty. It is not enough to constitute a promise that expectations are entertained; they must be

[1] Moral and Political Philosophy, Book iii., Chap. 15.

knowingly and voluntarily excited by ourselves. It is nothing worth, therefore, to affirm that because truth is expected when we seriously address our discourse to another, therefore we have tacitly promised to speak it, unless it can be shown that this expectation has been intentionally produced by our agency. We are not bound by any other expectations of men but those which we have authorized. It is idle, therefore, to pretend to a contract in the case. If Dr. Paley had pushed his inquiries a little farther, he might have accounted for this expectation, which certainly exists, independently of a promise, upon principles firmer and surer than any he has admitted in the structure of his philosophy. He might have seen in it the language of our nature proclaiming the will of our nature's God. It is surprising to what an extent this superficial theory of "contract" has found advocates among divines and moralists. "Upon the principles of natural reason," says South,[1] in a passage of which the extract from Paley may be regarded as an abridgment, "the unlawfulness of lying is grounded upon this, that a lie is properly a sort or species of injustice, and a violation of the right of that person to whom the false speech is directed; for all speaking, or signification of one's mind, implies, in the nature of it, an act or address of one man to another, it being evident that no man, though he does speak false, can be said to lie to himself. Now, to show what this right is, we must know that, in the beginnings and first establishments of speech, there was an implicit compact amongst men, founded upon common use and consent, that such and such words or voices, actions or gestures, should be means or signs whereby they would express or convey their thoughts one to another, and that men should be obliged to use them for that purpose; forasmuch as without such an obligation those signs could not be effectual for such an end. From which compact there arising an obligation upon every one so to convey his meaning, there accrues also a right to every one, by the same signs, to judge of the sense or meaning of

[1] Sermon on Falsehood and Lying, Prov. xii. 22.

the person so obliged to express himself; and consequently, if these signs are applied and used by him so as not to signify his meaning, the right of the person to whom he was obliged so to have done is hereby violated, and the man, by being deceived and kept ignorant of his neighbour's meaning, where he ought to have known it, is so far deprived of the benefit of any intercourse or converse with him."

If men once existed in a state of solitary independence, as destitute of language as of society, it is impossible to conceive how they could have established a mutual understanding and concerted the signs which were subsequently to be employed as the vehicles of thought. There must have been some mode of communication, or the convention in question becomes utterly impracticable. Whatever that mode might be, the obligation of veracity applied to it in order that it might be effectual, and an arrangement which presupposes, cannot be the source of, a duty. Men were either bound to represent their thoughts honestly to each other when they came together to frame an artificial language, or they were not. If they were previously bound, the obligation cannot spring from any agreement entered into at the time; if they were not, there is no security that the terms of the agreement express the intentions of the parties, and no evidence accordingly that any real promise was made. Such are the inconsistencies incident to all explanations of the origin of society and language which overlook the historical facts of the Bible. Man was evidently created a social being and with the gift of speech. He was as much adapted, when he came from the hands of God, to intercourse with his fellows by the possession of language as by the possession of those instincts, passions and affections which make the Home, the Family and the State indispensable to his progress and development. He was born in society and for society; it is not a condition which he has voluntarily selected from a calculation of its conveniences and comforts; it is the condition in which God has placed him, and from which he cannot be divorced.

Language is arbitrary in the sense that there is, except to a very limited extent, no natural analogy between sounds and the thoughts they represent; it is not arbitrary in the sense that it is purely the product of the human will; it is not an invention, but a faculty, and, like all other faculties, capable of improvement or abuse.

The account which Dr. Whewell gives, in his Elements of Morality,[1] of the obligation of veracity, though it is free from the paralogisms of Paley and South and the theory of contract, is not unencumbered with difficulties of its own. Among the springs of action he enumerates the need of a mutual understanding among men, speaks of this as a need rather than a desire, it being "rather a necessity of man's condition than an object of his conscious desire." " We see this necessity," he continues, " even in animals, especially in those which are gregarious. In their associated condition they derive help and advantage from one another, and many of them, especially those that live, travel or hunt in companies, are seen to reckon upon each other's actions with great precision and confidence. In societies of men this mutual aid and reliance are no less necessary than among beavers or bees. But in man this aid and reliance are not the work of mere instinct. There must be a mutual understanding by which men learn to anticipate and to depend upon the actions of each other. This mutual understanding presupposes that man has the power of determining his future actions, and that he has the power of making other men aware of his determination. It presupposes purpose as its matter and language as its instrument."

It is clear that Dr. Whewell had principally in view promises and contracts—those purposes of our own in regard to the future which have given rise to expectations in others in conformity with which they have adjusted their plans and regulated their conduct. Mutual understanding is a *necessity* only where deceit is an injury. There are cases of falsehood in which it would be hard to prove that any shock

[1] Book I., chap. ii., § 50.

is given to society, provided it were understood that the pre-
varication in these cases is not inconsistent with the strictest
integrity in those in which confidence is really important.
Upon Dr. Whewell's principles, the law of veracity is not
universal, embracing every instance and form in which one
man communicates ideas to another; it extends only to
those contingencies in which we have entered into virtual
engagements. He could convict jesting and foolish talking
of guilt only on the ground that they imperceptibly disturb
our love of truth and undermine the security of our faithfulness, and gradually introduce us into fraud and treachery.
They are not wrong upon his hypothesis essentially and
inherently, but only indirectly and contingently.

In the next place, it is not explained how this need of
mutual understanding operates as a spring of action. It is
denied to be a conscious desire; it is denied to be an instinct,
by which, I suppose, he means a blind craving of our nature.
What, then, is it? If it expresses simply a necessity of
our condition as social, we are either conscious of this necessity or we are not. If we are not conscious of it, it can
have no possible influence upon us. It will be to us as
though it existed not. If we are conscious of it, then it
must produce desire, and that desire must lead to expedients
to gratify it. Speaking the truth, as the means of satisfy-
ing this craving of our nature, would consequently be the
suggestion of reason. This, I think, is what the learned
author meant, although some expressions he has used are
hardly reconcilable with it. If so, the obligation of veracity is a deduction of the understanding from the circumstances in which we are placed. The end to be gained is
first distinctly suggested by a sense of need, and veracity is
enforced as the only conceivable expedient by which it can
be accomplished. Hence, the law of truth is not a primary
and fundamental datum of consciousness, but a secondary
and subordinate principle which requires some knowledge
of our social relations in order to its development. The

statement of these difficulties is a sufficient refutation of
the hypothesis.

The real ground upon which the obligation of this, as
ultimately the obligation of every other duty must be made
to rest, is the will of God as expressed in the constitution
of the human mind. Truth is *natural.* There are two
principles or laws impressed upon every man, by which he
is adapted to social intercourse, and which operate independently of any consciousness on his part of their subserviency
to the interests of society, and which manifest themselves in
the form of *dispositions*—one prompting him to speak the
truth himself, and the other to believe that others speak it.
No man ever tells a lie without a certain degree of violence
to his nature. Motives must intervene, of fear, or hope, or
vanity, or shame ; *temptations,* as in the case of all other
vices, must take place in order that the contradiction to our
nature and the whole current of our thoughts or feelings
involved in a falsehood may obtain. It is not the spontaneous native offspring of the soul, it is the creature of
passion and of lust. It is in consequence of this constitution of the mind, with reference to truth and social intercourse, that the expectation of which Dr. Paley speaks, as
always existing when we seriously address our discourse to
another, springs up in the breast. This expectation is only
the manifestation of our natural tendency to speak the truth
and to credit the statements of others. When we look at
ourselves we see that God has impressed upon our souls the
law of truth. We see that he has fitted us to trust at the
same time in others ; and though both dispositions are
indulged long antecedently to any knowledge of the important bearing of such elements of our being upon the
interests of society, yet the subsequent development of these
relations strengthens our attachment to truth, and enlarges
our views of the wisdom of God. The Author of our
nature has made provision for a mutual understanding
among men, and not left them under the influence of a
blind craving to make provision for themselves. Our

social affections might just as reasonably be ascribed to a vague desire of society, prompting to the invention of expedients for its indulgence, as our disposition to speak the truth to a vague craving for the interchange of thought. To those, therefore, who would ask, Why am I bound to speak the truth? I would briefly answer, Because it is the law of our nature; it is a fundamental datum of conscience, a command of God impressed upon the moral structure of the soul. It can be resolved into no higher principle; it is simple, elementary, ultimate. In this view of the case it deserves further to be remarked that the obligation is universal, and not restricted to promises or contracts. It is not only natural to fulfil the expectations we knowingly and voluntarily excite, but it is equally natural that in the use of signs to communicate ideas we should fairly and honestly represent the thoughts of our own minds. In every case nature prompts us to speak and expect the truth, and it is not until experience has taught us that our confidence is often abused that we learn to limit our credulity, and even then, "notwithstanding the lessons of caution communicated to us by experience, there is scarcely a man to be found," as Dr. Reid has properly remarked, "who is not more credulous than he ought to be, and who does not upon many occasions give credit to tales which not only turn out to be perfectly false, but which a very moderate degree of reflection and attention might have taught him could not well be true. The natural disposition is always to believe. It is acquired wisdom and experience alone that teach incredulity, and they very seldom teach it enough."

Having now explained the ground of the obligation of veracity, I proceed to consider the duties which are involved in the general law of sincerity.

This law is that the signs, whatever they may be, by which we intentionally communicate ideas should correspond as exactly as possible with the thoughts they are employed to represent.

1. The first thing here to be noted is that truth is not to

be restricted to speech. Language is not the only vehicle of thought. A greater prominence is given to it than to any other sign because it is the most common and important instrument of social communication. But the same rule of sincerity which is to regulate the use of it applies to all the *media* by which we consciously produce impressions upon the minds of others. Augustin defines a lie to be the false signification of a word for the purpose of deceit, and intimates that by the term *word* he means any and every significant sign, whether spoken or written, whether natural or artificial—gestures, actions, looks or ejaculations. It may be also added that the absence of any signs, or the omission to use them, may have the effect of suggesting thoughts, and when we neglect them from this consideration we are responsible for the effect produced. A lie, then, is compendiously "*any* false signification knowingly and voluntarily used," no matter what may be the instruments employed for the purpose. He who responds to the question of a traveller concerning the road by pointing in a wrong direction, who nods to a proposal which he does not mean to accept, who omits in a narrative a circumstance without which an erroneous judgment cannot but be formed in the case, or so arranges his facts as to lead naturally and justly to inferences that are false,—he who in these, or in any other ways, consciously misleads his neighbour is as really wanting in sincerity and as truly guilty of a lie as if he had deceived by words. Appearances kept up for the purpose of deceiving, such as a splendid equipage by one whose income is inadequate to the expense, hurry and bustle in a physician without patients, a multitude of papers by a lawyer without briefs, and all similar tricks for effect, belong to this species of dissembling. South thinks that though the principle is the same in each case, the term *lie* is distinctly applied to deception by words, and *simulation* or *hypocrisy* to deception by gestures, actions or behaviour. I apprehend, however, that *hypocrisy*, according to general usage, denotes only a particular species of this deception.

It refers to the personation of a character that does not
belong to us. We are hypocrites only as we pretend to be
that which we are not.

2. The application of the law in the case of parables,
fictions, tales and figurative language, such as hyberbole and
irony, is not to the details and subordinate statements, but
to the moral, which, as a whole, they are intended to illustrate. Dr. Paley has strangely enumerated these under the
head of *falsehoods which are not lies,* attaching them to the
same class with the disingenuous assertions of an advocate
in pleading a cause or with a servant's denial of his master.
But in these cases there is evidently, in no proper sense, any
falsehood at all. The fable, parable or tale, taken as a
whole, may be and is regarded as a species of proposition in
which the lesson to be inculcated is all that is strictly
affirmed. The rest is drapery, mere conceptions of the
imagination, intended to illustrate and place in commanding
lights the ultimate truth to be taught. They are not proposed as facts, but rather as the signs and representatives of
what might be facts. They are, in other words, only the
language in which the proposition is enounced. When a
man honestly believes the moral of his tale, whatever may
be its ingredients and subordinate circumstances, he is not
wanting in sincerity. The pictures of his fancy are not the
things which he affirms. If, however, he should invent a
story to enforce a proposition which he believes to be false,
he would then violate the obligation of veracity. It is only
where the end aimed at is contradictory to a man's own convictions that these contrivances of the imagination possess
either the form or matter of falsehood. Of course, if a man
should assert the details of a fable, parable or fiction as *facts,*
without believing them himself, he would be justly subject
to the imputation of lying, as he might be equally subject,
if he believed them, to the imputation of insanity.

3. There is a form of simulation which is resorted to for
the purpose of exciting curiosity, stimulating attention, conveying instruction or exploring and bringing to light what

otherwise might not be known. It is a species of interrogatory by action. It has the same effect on the mind as the asking of a question. When our Saviour made as though He would have gone farther, He effectually questioned His disciples as to the condition of their hearts in relation to the duties of hospitality. The angels, in pretending that it was their purpose to abide in the street all night, made the same experiment on Lot. This species of simulation involves no falsehood; its design is not to deceive, but to catechize or instruct. The whole action is to be regarded as a sign by which a question is proposed, or the mind excited to such a degree of curiosity and attention that lessons of truth can be successfully imparted. The command to Abraham to sacrifice his son involved a series of practical interrogatories to which no other form of proposing them could have elicited such satisfactory responses. The principle holds here which obtains in reference to fictions and fables. The action is only the dress of the thought, and where the purpose in view is honourable and just, no exceptions can be taken on the score of veracity to the drapery in which it is adorned. But when it has no ulterior object, when it is not in fact a sign, it is then to be reckoned as deceit. It is to be judged of simply as it is in itself—just as the details of a fiction, if represented absolutely and as facts, are to be regarded as departures from veracity. Even if capricious simulations were not, as they are, lies, they are so much like them that he who accustoms himself to indulge in this species of conduct must insensibly lose his impressions of the sacredness of truth, and forfeit that delicate sensibility to its claims upon which sincerity depends. It is dangerous to sport even on the verge of guilt. The least that can be said with any show of reason is, that unmeaning pretences are analogous to foolish talking and jesting, which are not convenient. It is especially important, in the education of children, that we allow ourselves in no conduct which may insensibly affect them with light thoughts of the evil of hypocrisy. The child who sees his parents frequently feigning without reason, or merely for amusement, will be a dull scholar in depravity if he should not speedily conclude that he also may feign when his interest or malice requires it.

4. The law of sincerity is not violated in those cases of silence or of partial and evasive information (which, however, must always be correct as far as it goes) in which the design is not deception, but concealment. There are things which men have a right to keep secret, and if a prurient curiosity prompts others officiously to pry into them, there is nothing criminal or dishonest in refusing to minister to such a spirit. Our silence or evasive answers may have the effect of misleading. That is not our fault, as it was not our design. Our purpose was simply to leave the inquirer, as nearly as possible, in the state of ignorance in which we found him: it was not to misinform, but not to inform at all. "Every man," says Dr. Dick, "has not a right to hear the truth when he chooses to demand it. We are not bound to answer every question which may be proposed to us. In such cases we may be silent, or we may give as much information as we please and suppress the rest. If the person afterward discover that the information was partial, he has no title to complain, because he had not a right even to what he obtained; and we are not guilty of a falsehood unless we made him believe, by something which we said, that the information was complete. We are at liberty to put off with an evasive answer the man who attempts to draw from us what we ought to conceal." This principle is certainly recognized in the Scriptures. When Jeremiah was interrogated of the princes in relation to the interview which he had with the king, he concealed the principal design of it, which was to recommend submission to the Chaldeans, and disclosed only the petition that the king would not remand him to Jonathan's house. Samuel was instructed by the Lord to act upon the same principle in order to avoid the danger to which he would be exposed from the resentment of Saul if the real purpose of his mission to Bethlehem, when he would go to anoint David, should be known.

"And Samuel said, How can I go? If Saul hear it, he will kill me. And the Lord said, Take an heifer with thee, and say, I am come to sacrifice to the Lord."

The principle, of course, can only be applied to those cases where we have a right to conceal; but all partial and evasive answers when we are bound to speak the whole truth, or when they are given for the purpose of deception, are inconsistent with veracity. Then a man does not *hide*, but *lie*.

It may be asked whether a direct falsehood is not lawful when it is uttered only for the purpose of concealment. Sir Walter Scott, it is well known, defended his denial to the Prince of Wales of his being the author of the Waverley Novels, on the ground that it was a matter which he was anxious to keep secret, and that he could not do it in any other way but by the course which he had pursued. In all such cases, however, the *immediate* end is deception; concealment is only a remote one. We intend to deceive in order to conceal. We do not *cover*, but *misrepresent* our mind, which can never be lawful, however important the ends it is intended to accomplish; and when these ends are incapable of being answered in any other way, we should take it as a clear intimation from Providence that we are required to abandon them. In the case just mentioned Scott might have been silent, might have changed the subject, might have protested against the question; and although such evasions might have been considered equivalent to a confession, yet a disclaimer on his part that he meant them in that light would have still left the matter in some degree of uncertainty. Guilt, in such cases, is not confined to the party who prevaricates or lies. He who asks impertinent questions is chargeable with the sin of putting a stumbling-block in his brother's way. He is a tempter to evil.

Having made these general explanations, which seemed to be necessary in order to an adequate comprehension of the subject, I proceed to indicate some of the modes in which the law of sincerity is evaded, after which I shall

discuss the question whether under any circumstances it can
be dispensed with; this being perhaps the most satisfactory
method of elucidating the nature and extent of its application—more definite certainly than vague statements of what
it requires, which at best are little more than repetitions of
the definition.

1. The light in which Aristotle treats of truth in his
Nichomachean Ethics[1] is that of simplicity of conduct, and
the extremes of which he regards it as the medium are vain-
boasting and self-disparagement. "There are men," says
he, "who arrogate to themselves good qualities of which
they are entirely destitute, and who amplify the good qualities of which they are possessed far beyond their real measure and natural worth. The ironical dissembler [I should
prefer to translate the word *self-disparager*], on the other
hand, either conceals his advantages, or, if he cannot conceal,
endeavours to depreciate their value, whereas the man of
frankness and plain dealing shows his character in its natural size; truth appears in all his words and actions, which
represent him exactly as he is, without addition and without diminution." There are forms in which these vices are
as common as they are disgusting. Some endeavour to
exaggerate their importance by pretending to an intimacy
with the great to which they are not entitled, and others to
depreciate the excellencies for which they are distinguished,
only to elicit flattery and praise. In both cases it is the
hypocrisy of vanity, and in both cases the actor is guilty
of a lie.

The most serious form of hypocrisy, however, is that in
which a man pretends to a character to which he is really a
stranger. No vice is more severely condemned in the New
Testament than this: "But woe unto you, Scribes and
Pharisees, hypocrites! for ye shut up the kingdom of
heaven against men; for ye neither go in yourselves, neither
suffer ye them that are entering to go in." This terrible
malediction from lips that were not given to the language

[1] Book iv., chap. 7.

of denunciation is repeated no less than seven times in the progress of a single discourse, and the most striking imagery, such as whited sepulchres, beautiful without but within full of dead men's bones and all uncleanness, is employed to depict the hatefulness of the sin. The only honest way of maintaining the appearance of virtue is to possess the reality. Every other method is a cheat.

2. The law of sincerity is as inconsistent with adulation and flattery as it is with hypocrisy. The hypocrite and flatterer belong to the same genus; one lies about himself, the other about his neighbour, but both are equally liars. Affability or courtesy, an inseparable element of refined and elegant manners, is as remote, as Aristotle long ago pointed out, from flattery on the one hand as from moroseness on the other. Persons of station and influence are apt to be surrounded with a crowd of sycophants, who vie with each other in concealing their defects, exaggerating their virtues and lauding their vices. In becoming an encomiast of sin one seems to reach the last point of degradation to which a rational being can be sunk, and yet it is the point to which all flattery tends, and which many a flatterer has reached. This vice is sometimes contracted from malice, from the wicked design of exposing the weak and credulous to ridicule, by possessing them with the belief that they are distinguished for qualities which do not belong to them; sometimes from selfishness, from the base desire of rendering the vanity of another subservient to our purposes and schemes; sometimes from weakness, from a sickly delicacy of temper which shrinks from giving pain or from incurring the resentment to which honest truth might give rise. There are degrees of malignity in the vice according to the motives and ends which prompt to it; but in every form it is a departure from truth, as well as a departure from that charity which meditates no wrong to another. "A man that flattereth his neighbour spreadeth a net for his feet."

3. There is another form of falsehood which in its effects is analogous to flattery, and in its nature is a species of

hypocrisy. It consists in pretensions to a friendship which is not felt. The world thinks so little of this kind of lying that, except in flagrant and aggravated cases, it hardly takes the trouble to censure it when exposed. It has caused friendship to come to be esteemed as little more than a name.

This vice is peculiarly hateful, as it gains a confidence which is too often prostituted to the ruin of the unsuspecting and credulous. It was in the mask of friendship that the Devil entered the garden and insinuated the lie which brought "death into the world, with all our woe;" in the mask of friendship Judas kissed his Master to betray Him; and in the mask of friendship Satan now comes to us as an angel of light to seduce us from our allegiance to God. There is no point of practical morality which needs more to be inculcated than the sacred duty of abstaining from every species of conduct or expression that would induce men to believe that we think more highly of them than we do. The customs of society are such that, without perpetual vigilance, we are liable to deceive our neighbours upon this point. The civilities of life should never be so exaggerated as to create the impression of extraordinary regard where extraordinary regard does not exist. The affectation of unusual sweetness of expression or blandness of manner; honeyed words; soft and insinuating tones; a lingering pressure of the hand; apparent reluctance to quit one's society,—all these and similar expedients are arrant lies if the victim of the tricks is, after all, nothing more than a stranger; and yet by such tricks the confidence of thousands is flattered out of them by knaves and cheats to their utter ruin. The vice is well called *perfidy*, and those who are guilty of it are emphatically children of the Devil. "Instruments of cruelty are in their habitations. O my soul, come not thou into their secret; unto their assembly, mine honour, be not thou united."

4. It is hardly necessary to add, after what has been said of the nature of sincerity, that equivocation is inconsistent with its claims. It consists either in an abuse of the am-

biguity of language or in partial statements of the truth,
for the purpose of producing an erroneous impression of the
whole. The promise of Temures to the garrison of Sebastia,
that if it would surrender not a drop of blood should be
shed, was grammatically susceptible of the meaning in which
he kept it, though the garrison understood it as conveying a
pledge of exemption from punishment. He was just as truly
guilty of a falsehood in burying them alive, though he shed
no blood, as if he had promised, in so many words, to spare
their lives. Words were not meant to conceal, but to convey thoughts; and if a man takes advantage of their am-
biguity to make a grammatical truth subservient to deceit,
he fails to represent his own thoughts. He speaks against
his mind. The idea which he excites in another is not the
idea which exists in himself.

The other mode of equivocation—by partial statements—is
liable to the same objection. It does not reproduce our own
convictions in another. Our minds are not read, touching
the matter in question, by our neighbour.

Equivocation may exist in action as well as in words.
We have an example in the case of Ananias and Sapphira.
Having sold their lands, they brought a part of the price
and laid it down at the Apostles' feet. They wished to produce the impression that they were as liberal and magnani-
mous as Barnabas and the other believers, who had sold
their possessions and devoted the whole to the service of the
Church. The language accordingly of their conduct was
that this is the *whole* price of the land. They uttered no
falsehood in words—they simply acted a cheat; and the
light in which God regards such equivocation is manifested
in the supernatural judgment which overtook them.

5. Mental reservations, when what is suppressed is not
obvious from the circumstances, or is not necessary to prevent deception, are downright lies. What is kept to one's
self is not *signified.* It is the signs which one *uses,* not those
which he suppresses, which convey his thoughts to another;
and if those which he *uses* are not in correspondence with

his convictions, he signifies falsely, and therefore lies. That form of reservation in which the suppressed circumstances are things to be taken for granted as known, provided they are understood at the time to be known, is no real reservation at all. It is only where what is suppressed is essential to the truth, and is suppressed for the purpose of deceit, that the reservation comes under the censure of the moralist. And such frauds cannot be too strongly rebuked. They are destructive of all confidence, of all intercourse by signs.

Dr. Paley says that there are two cases in which falsehoods are not criminal. The first is " where no one is deceived;" the second, " where the person to whom you speak has no right to know the truth, or, more properly, where little or no inconvenience results from the want of confidence in such cases." These exceptions are perfectly consistent with the theory of moral obligation which confounds virtue with expediency and duty with advantage. In that everything depends upon the *effect;* and where no appreciable injury results or evident utility obtains, it is right and proper to prevaricate with any principles or to dispense with any laws. But if there be such a thing as inherent and essential rectitude, if the distinctions betwixt right and wrong be permanent and unchanging, and if truth be one of the elements of immutable morality, the answer of Paley must be condemned by every unsophisticated heart.

1. In the first class of cases which he exempts from the operation of the law of sincerity he has fallen into the unaccountable mistake that the essence of a lie depends upon the effect actually produced. He confounds the falsehood with the deception which it occasions. The utmost that can be said, with any show of reason, is that the *intention* to deceive is necessary to guilt; but the *intention* of the speaker and the *effect* consequent upon it are very different things. The abandoned liar, whose character is known to the community, has reached a point of degradation at which no one thinks of relying upon his word; and yet it would be strange philosophy to say that because he had become incapable of de-

ceiving, he had therefore become incapable of lying, except by telling the truth. Augustin's definition, which is the one commonly adopted, introduces the *purpose* of deceit as all that is necessary to render a false signification a lie. Even this, as it seems to me, is going beyond what the truth of the case admits. The law of sincerity requires that a man who addresses his discourse to another should introduce him, as nearly as possible, into the condition of his own mind. He should represent, by whatever signs he employs, the precise state of his own feelings and convictions. The essence of a lie, consequently, must consist in a misrepresentation of one's self or in speaking against one's mind. "Speech was invented," says Thomas Aquinas, "for the purpose of expressing the conceptions of the heart; whenever, therefore, any one utters what is not in his heart, he utters what is not lawful." The *intention*, accordingly, which determines the species of the lie, and which gives it its essential or formal criminality, is not the intention to deceive another, though that is criminal and is generally the effect of falsehood, but the *intention* to misrepresent ourselves. "Where these three things concur," says Aquinas, "that an enunciation should be false, voluntarily made, and intended to deceive, there is found material falsehood, the thing asserted not being true; formal falsehood, there being a will to utter what is not true; and effective falsehood, there being a desire to impress it upon others." It must be borne in mind, however, that the essence of lying consists in formal falsehood, or a voluntary enunciation of what is not true; it derives its name from the circumstance that it consists in speaking against one's mind. If any one, consequently, utters a falsehood, believing it to be true, he himself is not guilty of lying, though the thing itself be materially false, as he had no intention of falsehood. What is beside the intention of the speaker cannot enter into the specific difference of the act. In like manner, if a man should utter a truth believing it to be a lie, he would be chargeable with the moral guilt of falsehood, that being the purpose of his will which determines the character of his utterance, though accidentally it happens to be true. This pertains to the *species* of falsehood. But the purpose to mislead another by deception does not pertain to the species, but to the *perfection* of lying. It is falsehood having its perfect work. In natural things, whatever has that which pertains to the constitution of a species is referred to that species, though some of the usual effects may be wanting. A heavy body may be suspended in the air and the law of gravity counteracted, yet because the descent which gravity is fitted to produce does not take place, it would be absurd to deny that the body in question is possessed of weight.

Hence, to determine the question whether a man has lied or not it is not necessary to inquire whether he has actually deceived another, but whether he has signified in contradiction to the thoughts, feelings or convictions of his mind. It is a matter of no consequence whether his falsehood has been *believed* or not. The moral character of *his* act does not depend upon his neighbour's acuteness or simplicity, but upon the purpose of his own heart. The intention to deceive is of course to be presumed where a man voluntarily and consciously misrepresents himself. If the signs which he employs are fitted to produce a given impression, and he knows that they are so fitted—if the impression in question is one that would always be produced where the signs are honestly employed—he is to be held guilty of *designing* to make it. But whatever might be the secret purpose of his soul, he is a liar before God if he knowingly and willingly utters, or in any other way signifies, what is false. This is the essence of the sin. Other circumstances may aggravate its malignity, but this determines its specific difference.

2. Dr. Paley is equally unfortunate in the principle upon which he exempts his second class of cases from the law of sincerity. The right of another to know the truth is not the ground of my obligation when I speak at all to speak nothing but the truth. It is the ground in many cases of

my obligation to speak,—that may be freely confessed; but if independently of this ground I choose upon any other considerations to open my lips, the law of sincerity must apply to my discourse. The absence of the right in question on the part of my neighbour can operate no farther than to justify me in being silent; it exempts me from all obligation to signify at all. But it by no means imparts to me a right to signify falsely. The two questions, whether I am bound to speak at all in a given case, and what I shall speak, are entirely distinct. The consideration of my neighbour's right may be important in determining the first; it is of no importance to the other, except as it may affect the extent of my communications. It is preposterous and absurd to confound the absence of a right to know the truth with the existence of a right to be cheated with a lie. The ground of obligation to signify nothing but truth when one signifies at all is that it *is* truth; it is the law under which alone I am at liberty to use signs in social intercourse. It might be questioned whether even upon considerations of expediency the principle of Dr. Paley ought not to be condemned. To say that a right to lie is the correlative of the absence of a right to know the truth, would seem to be equivalent to a very general dispensation with the law of sincerity. Each man must, in ordinary cases, determine for himself whether the right attaches to his neighbour or not, and as his veracity is suspended upon his opinions in relation to this point, no one could ever be sure that he was not deceived. How is a man to know that his neighbour deems him entitled to the truth? From his neighbour's declaration? But that declaration has no value unless it is previously known that the right in question is conceded. It may be one of those things about which, in his judgment, another has no right to know the truth. Hence, Paley's law would obviously be the destruction of all confidence. How much nobler and safer is the doctrine of the Scriptures and of the unsophisticated language of man's moral constitution, that truth is obligatory on its own account, and that he who undertakes to signify to another, no matter in what form, and no matter what may be the right in the case to know the truth, is bound to signify according to the convictions of his own mind! He is not always bound to speak, but whenever he does speak he is solemnly bound to speak nothing but the truth. The universal application of this principle would be the diffusion of universal confidence. It would banish deceit and suspicion from the world, and restrict the use of signs to their legitimate offices.

DISCOURSE V.

FAITHFULNESS.

THE second branch of practical truth, which we have denominated Faithfulness, consists in making our actions
correspond to our professions, in performing our engagements,
and fulfilling the expectations which we have by any means
knowingly and voluntarily excited. Cicero[1] makes faith
the fundamental principle of justice, and derives the word
in Latin from the correspondence it exacts betwixt words
and deeds. The English term is said to be the third person singular of the indicative mood of an Anglo-Saxon
verb signifying to engage, to covenant, to contract. The
definition, however, extracted by Horne Tooke from this
etymology, " that which one covenanteth or engageth," is obviously inconsistent with the usage of the language. Faithfulness obtains not in the *making*, but in the keeping, of
covenants. It is not the *saying*, but the *doing* of what we
have said, that constitutes, as Cicero suggests, the very
essence of the virtue. *Quia fiat quod dictum est* contains
the substance of a good definition, whatever may be said
of the accuracy of the philosophy.

The engagements of men to which faithfulness extends

---

[1] Off., i. 7, 23. Fundamentum autem justitiæ est fides, id est, dictorum
conventorumque constantia et veritas. Ex quo, quamquam hoc videbitur
fortasse cuipiam durius, tamen audeamus imitari Stoicos, qui studiose
exquirunt, unde verba sint ducta, credamusque, quia *fiat*, quod dictum est,
appellatam fidem.

may be embraced under the heads of Promises, Pledges and Vows. These three classes, in their relations to each other, are an instance of moral climax, and furnish a beautiful illustration of the ascending scale of moral obligation. The pledge is more solemn than the promise, and the vow more solemn than the pledge. The peculiarities which distinguish the pledge and vow from an ordinary promise impart an additional sacredness to the duty. They are species of which it is the genus; they include consequently all that it includes, and something characteristic of themselves; and as the differences by which they are distinguished from it and from each other involve moral elements of the highest importance, there must be a corresponding solemnity of obligation and a corresponding malignity of guilt in case of transgression. The pledge turns upon a point of honour, and stakes a man's reputation for integrity upon compliance with his engagement. As the whole virtue of a female is summed up in her chastity, so the whole character of the man for probity and uprightness is summed up in the single instance of redeeming his pledge. To break a pledge, therefore, is not only unjust, but disgraceful. The vow is of the nature of an oath; it is an act of religious worship, and to disregard it is to be guilty of irreverence to God. There is fraud in all breaches of engagement, whether of promises, pledges or vows, that being the very essence of unfaithfulness; but to break a promise is simply fraudulent, to break a pledge is infamous, and to break a vow is profane. He who violates a promise tramples upon truth and justice, he who violates a pledge tramples upon character, and he who violates a vow tramples upon God.

In illustrating the duty of faithfulness I shall begin with promises, and restrict myself to two points—their definitions and the grounds of their obligation.

I. According to the ordinary acceptation of the term, the essence of a promise consists in the peculiar mode of signifying, to the exclusion of all reference to the matter or thing signified. Whenever by the voluntary use of signs, whe-

ther verbal or otherwise, we knowingly excite expectations
in the mind of another, whatever may be the nature of the
things expected, we are said to promise. The etymology of
the word has perhaps contributed to the currency of this
meaning. It is a paronym of *promittere*, to send ahead, as
if the prominent idea were the projection of the mind of
another into the future. *Qui pollicentur*, says Vossius, *ver-
bis aliquem in longum mittant, ut qui non tam faciant quam
aliquando se facturos recipiant.*

If the definition of a promise is to be restricted exclusively to the mode of signifying, it is manifest that promises are not essentially obligatory. Whether they shall be
binding or not is an accidental circumstance. There is
nothing in themselves, nothing in their own nature, considered simply as promises, which can give rise to the obligation. They may or may not do so, but when they do so it
is not because they are promises, but because of other considerations. This statement, though a legitimate deduction
from the definition in question and from the loose language
of ordinary life, is in open and flagrant contradiction to the
common feeling of the race. There is not a deeper or more
pervading sentiment than that of the sacredness of covenants. The common sense of men is always right, though
language does not always adequately represent it. There is
a distinction in the signification of words analogous to that
between the spontaneous and reflective processes of reason.
A philosopher, therefore, should not look to the meaning
which floats upon the surface, and which a term has received
from accidental circumstances; he should penetrate into the
hearts of men and find out the meaning which has real
emphasis there. That is its true signification, and the one
to which he should restrict it, which without reflection finds
an echo in the soul. In the case before us the associations
which are instantly awakened by the term are all of a solemn and sacred character. Its primary emphatic reference
is only to the class of declarations which are felt to be obligatory. It has been applied to others in consequence of the

palpable resemblance in form, but this is a reflective application, which, as it does not represent, so it does not disturb
the spontaneous feelings which cluster around the word.
It is still univocal to the heart. If, then, in conformity with
the real convictions of mankind, nothing can be regarded as
strictly and properly a promise which is not essentially
obligatory, the definition must include something more than
the mode of signifying. It must also take account of the
matter. As that is not to be considered as a deed in law—
though it may be loosely called so—which conveys no right,
so that should not be regarded as a promise, in the ethical
sense, which creates no duty. It may have the form, but
not the substance—the appearance, but not the reality.
Those semblances of the thing in which the language of a
promise is employed, but in which the life of a promise is
not found, I would call *apparent* promises, while those which
create obligation and give rise to rights I would denominate
real. Then the proposition would be universal that all real
promises are binding, and binding precisely because they
are promises; and all the cases in which divines and casuists
have held them to be void could be explained at once upon
the simple principle that they are not cases of promises at
all. They are only counterfeit coin. They have the shape,
the stamp, the appearance of the true currency, but they
want the gold. I would therefore define a real promise
as any form of voluntary signification which has a known
tendency to excite an expectation in the mind of another in
regard to a matter which is possible and right. Here the
mode of signifying and the thing signified, the matter and
the form, both enter into the specific difference. It is not
enough that expectations are excited, or means employed
which are suited to excite them; the things expected must
be lawful in themselves and within the competency of him
that promises. But we can best vindicate the propriety of
the definition by a brief examination of its parts:

1. *Any mode of voluntary signification, without limitation
to any particular class of signs.* This includes tacit as well

as express promises. It is obviously indifferent by what means thought is communicated: the important thing is that it be actually done. To restrict promises to words is to make them the only language of the mind, to the exclusion of actions, gestures and signs, which may be equally made the vehicle of thought and the instruments of exciting expectation.

2. The signification must be *voluntary*, otherwise the promise is not a moral act, and cannot be attributed to him who makes it.

3. *Which has a known tendency to excite expectation.* Paley makes the essence of a promise depend on the fact that expectations are excited. This is to resolve the cause into the effect. The promise must be conceived as *existing* before expectations can be conceived as produced. The fact of their production depends not upon the fact that a promise has been made, but that a promise has been believed, and faith in the author is essential to the reality and obligation of a promise; it is not simply his own act which binds the agent, but the effect it has produced. It would follow, too, that a liar could not make a promise, because he could not create expectation. The promise is clearly the act of the man that makes it, and as it comes from him independently of any influence upon others, it possesses every element that is necessary to a perfect obligation. It is indifferent whether it is believed or not; all that is important is that, if believed, it should give rise to expectation—it should be a cause suited to produce the effect, whether it succeeds in doing so or not. The author must *know* that it has this tendency. He must understand the import of his signs, or they would not convey the *thoughts* of his mind. The expectations which the signs are fitted to excite will always be, with an honest man, the expectations he aims to produce. His language will convey his real meaning. But if he is disposed to be dishonest and evasive, he is held responsible for the known tendencies of the cause which he has put in operation. The rule of Paley, that a promise is always to be interpreted in the sense in

which the promiser apprehended at the time that the promisee received it, results immediately from the definition we have given.

4. I have ventured to add to the definition, *in regard to a matter which is possible and right.* These, it is universally conceded, are conditions of the obligation of a promise. No man can be bound to do what it is physically impossible that he can do, or what contradicts the principles of right. It can obviously never be his duty to do wrong, and just as little can it be his duty to exercise a power which has never been imparted to him. If he was made a man, he can only be required to do the work of a man. Now, as all the other cases in which promises are not binding may be explained by showing that they are not promises at all, that something is wanting to complete them, or that they have been formally cancelled and annulled—as they are confessedly apparent and not real—it would contribute to simplify the whole subject if those which are impossible and unlawful were reduced to the same category. Any man who will take the trouble to examine Paley's enumeration of the cases in which promises are void, will see that, with the exception of the impossible and unlawful, the promise is either defective in form or has ceased to exist. A promise before acceptance—that is, before notice to the promisee—is manifestly no promise, because it wants the necessary element of signification. It is, as Paley says, nothing more than a resolution of the mind. Promises released by the promisee have just as manifestly ceased to exist. The right which was created has been relinquished, and the obligation has expired with it. Erroneous promises are not promises, because their being was contingent—it was suspended upon a condition which has confessedly failed. If now we make possibility and lawfulness essential to the being, as they are to the obligation of a promise, the proposition would be unlimited—that all real promises are binding, and that those are only apparent, only shadows and semblances, which entail no obligation of performance. These apparent promises would then be reduced

to two classes—those which are defective in form, embracing the three last heads of Paley, and those which are defective in matter, embracing his three first heads.

II. The next point to be considered is the ground of the obligation of promises.

The advantages of good faith are so palpable and manifest, it is so indispensable to the very existence of society, that the utilitarian makes out a very plausible case in resolving the duty of it into considerations of expediency. Paley has made the best of the argument. He has set in a very clear light not only the importance but the necessity of confidence, and then concludes that what we cannot do without we must have, simply because we cannot do without it. But the truth is, its importance depends upon its rectitude. Society is the union of moral and intelligent beings, and it is *because* they are *moral* that virtue is their security and happiness. It is the law of their nature, and of course is the condition of their prosperity and well-being.

Without detracting, therefore, in the least from what Paley has said upon the utility of confidence, we proceed to show that the real ground upon which promises are binding is, that they involve moral elements which are the immediate data of conscience. These elements are the principles of truth and justice. A man is bound to keep his promise from the twofold consideration that his own veracity and the rights of another are at stake.

1. The law of sincerity requires that the promiser should signify the purpose precisely as it exists in his own mind. He cannot mean one thing and say another without falsehood. This law, however, requires nothing more than the honest expression of present intentions.

2. But the law of truth goes farther; it requires that a man's words shall correspond to the reality of things. It is not enough, in regard to past facts, that a man be honest and sincere in the declarations which he makes; he must have used all diligence to guard against deception and mistake. If what we have called the remote matter of truth

be wanting, he is culpable unless his mistake arises from
causes beyond his control.   The same principle holds in
regard to future facts.   The event must correspond to our
words, unless it can be shown that though we honestly believed that it would correspond when we made the declaration, it has failed to do so through no fault of ours.   The
language of a promise is absolute and assertory; it positively affirms two things—a present intention and the continuance of that intention until the thing is done.   It
declares that a thing *shall* be, and as its existence depends
upon himself, the promiser is bound to realize the fact at
the appointed time.   He is bound to make things consistent
with his words.   Hence, he who fails to keep a promise is
universally detested as a liar, not because he is supposed to
have been insincere at the time of making it, but because
the thing has not taken place according to his word.   He is
responsible for the want of material truth, because it was
clearly in his power to produce it.

3. But what particularly enforces the obligation of a
promise is the right, created by the expectation it excites, to
have it fulfilled.   It is distinguished from a simple resolution in that it does not terminate upon ourselves.   It extends
to another party, and gives him a claim of justice which he
did not possess before.   Hence, a breach of promise is not only
a lie, but a fraud.[1]   The connection of rights with promises
is clearly discoverable in the case of contracts.   There the
engagement is mutual, but the transaction is only a recipro-
cation of promises; no moral elements enter into it which
do not enter into every other promise.   Now, there is nothing of which the parties to a contract are more distinctly
conscious than that they have a right to demand from each
other the fulfilment of their stipulations.   It is true that the

---

[1] We should remember that when we bind ourselves by a promise to
give any good thing to another, or to do anything for the benefit of
another, the right of the thing promised passes over from us to the person
to whom the promise is made, as much as if we had given him a legal
bond with all the formalities of signing and sealing; we have no power to
recall or reverse it without his leave."—*Watts' Sermon on Philippians* iv. 8.

law recognizes the right only in the case of valuable consideration. But the design of the distinction is to protect men from the consequences of rash and ill-considered acts. The presumption is, that what has been done without a proper motive has been done thoughtlessly and hastily. What shows that this is the spirit of the law is the fact that it always presumes a consideration where the promise has been made under such sanctions as to imply deliberation. There is no essential difference in so far as they are promises, and consequently in so far as moral obligation is concerned, between the *nudum pactum* of the law and those contracts which it undertakes to enforce. The consideration is not the source of the right; it is only the *cause* of the promise that gives the right. The consideration is a guarantee that the man has promised with his eyes open—that he knew what he was doing. The law interposes it as a security to itself that it shall not oppress the weak.

In the case of promises to do unlawful or impossible things there can obviously be no right on the part of the promisee to demand a fulfilment. It is a contradiction in terms that he can have a right to make his neighbour do wrong, and a flagrant absurdity that a creature can exact from his fellow what even God cannot enjoin. But while there is no injustice in the violation of these promises, there is enormous fraud in making them when the unlawfulness and impossibility are known at the time. The man shows himself reckless of truth and reckless of his neighbour's right. He manifests a contempt of veracity and justice. He is guilty of the same species of crime as that of him who solemnly pretends to transfer the property of another, or who knowingly circulates counterfeit coin, or who forges a note or a bill of exchange. As in other cases the falsehood and fraud consist in *breaking*, here they consist in *making* the promise. The crime is the same, but it dates from a different point. The same eternal principles of right which proclaim as with a voice of thunder, Thou shalt keep all real promises, just as solemnly command, Thou shalt make no unlawful engagements. In cases in which the unlawfulness and impossibility were not known at the time of making the promise, it may be fairly presumed that the promise was tacitly conditioned by them, and though there may be rashness, there is nothing of fraud in engagements made upon mistake. The implied condition has failed, and the promise is at an end.

Before dismissing the subject of promises there are two questions of casuistry which deserve a moment's consideration, and which may be regarded as a test of the principles we have maintained.

The first is, whether extorted promises are binding. The second is, whether when a promise proceeds upon an unlawful condition, and the condition has been fulfilled, the promise is to be kept—that is, whether there can ever be a real promise which is unlawfully conditioned.

1. As to extorted promises, the only point to be settled is the subjective condition of the agent.[1] Did he voluntarily signify, and did he know the import of the signs he employed? If he was in such a state of agitation and alarm that he could not command the use of his faculties—if, in other words, he was deprived for the time of the essential elements of moral agency—he could no more be responsible for his acts than an idiot or a lunatic. But if he *knew* what he was doing, no violence of fear, no external pressure, can exempt him from responsibility. The act was voluntary, though not chosen for itself. The man was in circumstances which led him to prefer it as the least of two evils. He therefore in a moral sense deliberately promised, and the obligation is the same as in all other cases. The true security against being drawn into an engagement which we are subsequently reluctant to perform is that firm reliance upon the providence of God which enables us to look upon danger with contempt, or to regard nothing as a danger which does not shake our claim upon the Divine protection. Let

---

[1] See on this subject, besides the common treatises, Taylor's Rule of Conscience, book iv., chap. i., rule 7.

the heart be established by confidence in Him, and then there is no ground for the fear of evil tidings. The preservation of integrity should be superior to all other considerations, and it is a miserable confession of weakness that the love of life or limb has been stronger than the love of virtue. No Christian man should ever be prevailed on by the servile motive of fear to make engagements which his sense of propriety condemns. Why should he fear who has the arms of the Almighty to sustain him? What shield like that of a good conscience and the favour of God? Of all men the true Christian should exemplify the description of the heathen poet:

> Justum ac tenacem propositi virum
> Non civium ardor prava jubentium,
> Non vultus instantis tyranni
> Mente quatit solida, neque Auster
> Dux inquieti turbidus Hadriæ,
> Nec fulminantis magna manus Jovis.
> Si fractus illabatur orbis
> Impavidum ferient ruinæ.

Those circumstances in which cowardice yields and puts in the plea of extortion constitute the occasions on which the Christian hero may illustrate the magnanimity of his principles. Virtue becomes awful when it subordinates to itself the whole external world. A good man struggling with the storms of fate, unshaken in his allegiance to God, and steady in his purpose never to be seduced into wrong, is the noblest spectacle which the earth can present. There is something unutterably grand in the moral attitude of him who, with his eye fixed upon the favour of God, rises superior to earth and hell, and amid the wrecks of a thousand barks around him steers his course with steadiness and peace.

2. To the other question concerning the effect of an unlawful condition upon the validity of a promise, I am constrained to return a very different answer from that which has been given by most recent writers whom I have been

able to consult.[1] Paley says,[2] " it is the *performance* being
unlawful, and not any unlawfulness in the subject or motive
of the promise, which destroys its validity : therefore, a bribe
after the vote is given ; the wages of prostitution ; the reward
of any crime after the crime is committed, ought, if promised, to be paid. For the sin and mischief, by this supposition, are over ; and it will be neither more nor less for the
performance of the promise." " It is sometimes made a
question," says Dr. Whewell,[3] " supposing such an informal
contract immorally made, whether, when the immoral end is
answered, it is a duty to perform the rest of the contract ; for
instance, if a person were elected to an office of public trust
on promise of sums of money to the electors, whether, after
the election, it is his duty to pay these sums. We may remark that the question here is not what he is to do as an
innocent man, for by the supposition he is a guilty one,
having been concerned in an immoral bargain. If the question be, what is he to do as a repentant man, convinced of
his guilt and wishing henceforth to do what is right, the
answer is that he must pay. There is no reason why he
should add to the violation of his absolute duty the violation
of his relative duty to the promisees. If in his repentance
he wishes not to complete an immoral transaction, he is to
recollect that the immoral transaction is completed by his
election. If he wish to mark his hatred of the offence, he
may signify his meaning more clearly by expressing his
repentance and paying the money than by keeping it, which
may be interpreted as adding avarice and falsehood to the
violation of public duties."

Upon these statements I have to remark—1, that Paley's
solution is inconsistent with the principles of his own philosophy. The effect of keeping such promises is to encourage

---

[1] I am gratified in being able to state that Dr. Adams, late President
of Charleston College, is an honourable exception. See his Moral Philos.,
p. 210.

[2] Mor. Phil., B. iii., Pt. i., c. 5.

[3] Elements of Morality, book iii., chap. 15, § 386.

the making of them, and upon the doctrine of general consequences—the evil of the example—they ought not to be kept.
" The sin and mischief " are not over.   If it were universally
felt and acted on that such engagements were not binding,
there would soon be an end to them.   It is the very doctrine
of Paley and Whewell that gives them currency in the world.

2. In the next place, Dr. Whewell's solution proceeds upon
a distinction between relative and absolute duties which is
purely fictitious and arbitrary.   He affirms that in the case
of an immoral promise there is an absolute duty to break it.
" In all such cases the promiser by his promise has rejected
his moral nature, and can only resume it by repudiating his
own act."   But there is a relative duty to the promisee to
keep it.   Now, if I owe a relative duty to the promisee, he
has a moral claim upon me, in the language of Dr. Whewell,
in which a moral claim is equivalent to an imperfect right.
There is, consequently, a collision of absolute and relative
duty.   If, therefore, a man keeps his promise, he does his
duty and yet sins ; or if he breaks his promise, he does his
duty and sins ; that is, the same act is both right and
wrong at the same time.   The absurdity is intolerable, and
yet it cannot be avoided without repudiating the distinction
in question.   The true state of the case is, that the absolute
duty is the *only* duty involved, and the effect of it is to prevent the rise of the relative duty which ensues upon a lawful
promise.   It is the absolute principles of right which determine obligation in the concrete instances of life.   There
never can be a duty, relative or absolute, to do a *wrong*
thing.   It is a contradiction in terms.   No man can ever
have a claim upon another for a violation of the eternal principles of right.   As, then, the existence of a relative duty
depends, in every case, upon the lawfulness of the promise,
Dr. Whewell, instead of resolving the difficulty, has quietly
begged the question.   He has assumed that there *is* a relative duty to the promisee, when that is the very point in dis-
pute, and vindicates his assumption by maintaining that in
all cases of immoral promises it exists, though, when the per-

formance is unlawful, the superior importance of the absolute duty supersedes it.

3. To me it seems that the true answer is, that an unlawful condition renders the promise absolutely null and void. That condition, in the language of the schools, is no moral entity; and *ex nihilo nihil fit* is as true in morals as physics. The man who stipulated to perform it was confessedly not bound; the other party had, and could have, no right or claim upon him. His act, therefore, has no moral value. The promise and its fulfilment, however, are only parts of one and the same process. If now, at the time of making the unlawful stipulation, the maker was not bound by it, the other party was equally free from obligation in relation to his promise. The promiser was bound only upon the supposition that the promisee was bound. Now, if the making and fulfilment of a promise are parts of the same *act*, and no obligation accrued at the time of making, it is clear that none can ever subsequently arise. The moral relation of the parties undergoes no changes.

4. It should further be recollected that to maintain the validity of such promises is completely to reverse the cardinal principle of moral government. It is to reward the wicked and to punish the righteous. There is something inexpressibly revolting in either giving or receiving the wages of iniquity. I cannot conceive of a position in which a man more openly and flagrantly sets at defiance the eternal rule of justice, or more shockingly travesties the moral administration of his God, than when he dispenses favours to the guilty upon the ground that they are guilty. This attitude of bold contradiction to the law of the Divine government is enough to brand with enormity the doctrine which justifies it. He cannot be right who mocks instead of imitating God. I have no doubt that the moral principle which I am here repudiating, and which is so generally maintained, is the prolific parent of infamy, outrage and crime. It is a devil whose name is legion. Let it be cast out from society, and many a man who has been the victim of its power will

be found clothed and in his right mind sitting at the feet of Jesus.

One consideration which serves to uphold this species of promises is the apprehension that if, when the unlawful condition has been performed the other party should refuse to execute his engagements, he will be exposed to the imputation of mean and interested motives. He would not be likely to receive any credit for a high sense of integrity. If he was not too conscientious to begin the sin, the presumption would be that it was something besides conscience which kept him from completing it. This equivocal position is the penalty which repentance must pay for the crime. It is a grievous cross, but it is a cross that must be borne. It is a memorial of transgression which serves at once to promote severity to ourselves and charity to others—a broken limb or a bone out of joint that keeps one in constant recollection of his fall.

I cannot dismiss this subject of promises without alluding to the peculiar interest which attaches to it, in the mind of the true believer, in consequence of the prominence which is given to the promises of God in the dispensation of the Gospel. The faithfulness of Jehovah is our only hope; and for the purpose of alluring our confidence, as well as illustrating His own grace, He deals with His creatures in the way of covenant. He condescendingly gives them a right which emboldens their access to the throne of grace. The promises, all Yea and Amen in Christ Jesus, are the sure warrant that they shall not be received with coldness nor sent empty away. Hardly a blessing is bestowed which is not apprehended in some promise before it is enjoyed in experience. A faithful and covenant-keeping God—these are the precious titles by which a sinner loves to recognize the God and Father of our Lord Jesus Christ. The Gospel is nothing but a great charter of promises; and that man must renounce his inheritance in the covenant of grace and abjure the hope of everlasting life who can think or speak lightly of what the blessed God has sanctified by His own example. In reverencing the sacredness of promises we reverence Him who is emphatically a God to sinners only when in faith they apprehend His covenant. In the preciousness of His promises we have an illustration of the moral value of faithfulness; and the fidelity which we delight to attribute to Him we should endeavour to imitate in all our own engagements. Be ye perfect, even as your Father in heaven is perfect. Whatsoever things are true, think on these things.

PLEDGES.

Pledges, under the Roman law, were properly securities for the payment of a debt. The thing pledged was put into the possession of the creditor, with a right to sell it and indemnify himself against the loss in case the debtor failed to comply with his contract. If, for example, a man borrowed money and deposited his jewels with the lender in token that he would repay the sum, the jewels became a pledge or pawn. In war and among public enemies the security for the faithful execution of a treaty or the performance of any specific stipulations was called a hostage. Whatever was pledged or pawned was, of course, possessed of such value that the desire to redeem it would be likely to be stronger than any inducements to violate faith. The fundamental notion of a pledge, therefore, is that of a security—a protection to the promisee against injury or loss. In bargains of sale or contracts of debt the thing pledged was always something that the creditor might sell. In treaties among hostile armies, hostages were usually persons of consequence, whose redemption was of greater importance than any incidental advantages that might accrue from breach of engagement. In either case, the pledge was a distinct, tangible, palpable thing, and of such value as to be a real guarantee of good faith. Transferred from bargains and treaties to a peculiar and solemn form of promises, the pledge still retains its fundamental meaning of security, but ceases to be a tangible commodity. In these cases it is a man's honour which he puts in pawn as a guarantee of the faithful execution of his promise.

The language of a pledge is, I renounce all claims to integrity and honour, I am willing to be excluded from society, to be stripped of character, to be an object of contempt and detestation, if I am found wanting in fidelity to my engagements.

The faith which is pledged under such sanctions cannot be violated without aggravated guilt. Character is not a thing to be sported with, infamy and disgrace not trifles to be laughed at; and he who deals with honour as a bauble will experience a penalty that may well make him tremble. It cannot be too earnestly inculcated upon the young that to break a pledge is apt to be followed by the total ruin of one's virtue. Transgression is not a transitory thing. The single act is soon done and over, but it leaves an influence behind, which, like the adder's poison, may grow and operate and spread until it reaches the seat of life and triumphs in the ruin of its victim. No act of the will—it is an indestructible and fearful law of our being—ever passes away without leaving its mark upon the character. There is a double tendency in every voluntary determination—one to propagate itself, the other to weaken or support, according to its own moral quality, the general principle of virtue. Every sin, therefore, imparts a proclivity to other acts of the same sort, and disturbs and deranges at the same time the whole moral constitution; it tends to the formation of special habits, and to the superinducing of a general debility of principle which lays a man open to defeat from every species of temptation. The extent to which a single act shall produce this double effect depends upon its intensity, its intensity depends upon the fullness and energy of will which will enter into it, and the energy of will depends upon the strength of the motives resisted. An act, therefore, which concludes an earnest and protracted conflict, which has not been reached without a stormy debate in the soul, which marks the victory of evil over the love of character, sensibility to shame, the authority of conscience and the fear of God,—an act of this sort concentrates in itself the essence of all the single determinations which preceded it, and possesses a power to generate a habit and to derange the constitution equal to that which the whole series of resistances to duty, considered as so many individual instances of transgression, is fitted to impart. By one such act a man is impelled with an amazing momentum in the path of evil. He lives years of sin in a day or an hour. It is always a solemn crisis when the first step is to be taken in a career of guilt, against which nature and education or any other strong influences protest. The results are unspeakably perilous when a man has to fight his way into crime. The victory creates an epoch in his life. From that hour, without a miracle of grace, he is a lost man. The earth is strewed with wrecks of character which were occasioned by one fatal determination at a critical point in life, when the will stood face to face with duty, and had to make its decision deliberately and intensely for evil. That act threw the whole energy of being into the direction of sin. A young man has been trained in a righteous horror of gambling; he looks upon cards or dice with shuddering and dread. His whole soul is set against them. In an ill-omened hour he is tempted to play. The associations of childhood, his father's counsels, his mother's warnings, a sister's love, the convictions of his own judgment, the fearful consequences of the crime both in this world and that which is to come, every moral energy which conscience, religion and the love of character can summon, rise up to protest against the deed. He is staggered, he hesitates, he almost resolves to flee the temptation. But a spell is on him, the seducer pursues him, the conflict is renewed, he is in agony, and at last resolves in desperation and madness to terminate the struggle—he *plays*. From that time his character is fixed, the man is ruined.

To break a pledge is a critical act of the same kind. It is an act of concentrated potency for evil. It is a victory after a severe contest, and, in the triumph of evil, sensibility to shame and tenderness of conscience have been paralyzed or lost. The man feels that he is disgraced and degraded, and gives himself up to infamy and vice without a further struggle. Character is gone, and all motive for honourable effort has ceased to exist. As in the case of the female who has lost her chastity, his virtue has perished with his honour. It is a solemn thing to stake character upon the hazard of a single act, and he who has done it should feel that nothing less than the whole moral history of his being is involved in the issue. When the pledge is apprehended in its true significancy and relations, and the natural effects of a breach of it, according to the fixed principles of human nature, are duly appreciated, it will be seen to be one of those critical obligations which should be approached with somewhat of the awful reverence that belongs to the oath. It should never be made cheap. It is a *security*, and should only be resorted to on important occasions where important interests are at stake. But once made in regard to a matter which is possible and right, a man should die rather than forego it. Death is tolerable, but real dishonour cannot be borne.

Sacred as the pledge is, however, it can never justify wrong. After what has been said upon the subject of promises, to which the pledge generically belongs, it would be unnecessary to add anything here, were it not that the feelings of the young are apt to mislead them upon this point, and betray them into contradictions, which, always a snare, may terminate in permanent injury to character. The alternative seems to be dishonour or an unlawful act. Both are evils, and upon the principle of choosing the least an individual instance of transgression is preferred to a general shock of the moral sensibilities. The young man says, I had rather do this particular unlawful act than sacrifice the whole security for good which I find in a delicate regard for reputation. In this predicament students in college are very often involved. They enter into combinations against legiti-

mate authority under the sanctions of a pledge. They feel
that their honour is at stake, and that their faith must be
redeemed at whatever sacrifice to their own prospects, the
wishes of their parents or the prosperity of the Institution
against which they have conspired. The feeling—that of the
sacredness of honour—is a noble one, and should not be
rudely shocked. But the point is, that true honour in this case
requires that the pledge should be broken. It was a grievous sin to make it, but, having been made, nothing remains
but the duty which extends to every instance of transgression—of immediate repentance. The evil must be undone.
The man who has taken a wrong step should instantly
retrace it. There can, in the nature of things, be no obligation to persevere. Unlawful pledges, like unlawful promises, create no rights; and as the attempt to give a security for
evil only deepens the crime, the pledge is only a counterfeit
stipulation of honour. The principle which would attach
dishonour to the breach of such unlawful engagements, if
legitimately carried out, would unhinge the entire system
of morals. It assumes that man can set aside the law of
God, that the stern prohibitions of eternal rectitude can be
changed into transient, commands by the will of a feeble
creature, that the word of man may become superior to the
word of his Maker. No; let God be true and every man a
liar, and when He speaks let us promptly obey, whatever
may have been our previous engagements to evil. The
effects which result from the breach of a lawful pledge, and
which render it so critical, cannot obtain in this case. The
spirit which here operates is the spirit of repentance; the
act is an act of virtue, and its tendency consequently is to
strengthen the general principle of virtue. To keep the
pledge, however, as an act of transgression, has all the influences which essentially inhere in sin. We say, therefore,
confidently to the young, Be cautious never to be entangled
in engagements of this sort, but if in an evil hour you have
been seduced into them, take the first opportunity of reassert-
ing your allegiance to right.

There is not a more touching proof of God's condescension to the weakness of His creatures than the use of the pledge on His part to assure our hearts of the immutability of His counsel. His promises, though felt to be Yea and Amen in Christ Jesus, appeal to considerations less personal and distinct—the abstract principles of truth and justice; but the pledge is an appeal to His honour, or, in the language of Scripture, to His glory, which stands in the same relation to Him that honour does to us. We cannot disbelieve without the most revolting blasphemy when God puts His character in pawn for His word. He addresses us on a ground which comes home to us with peculiar power. He transfers to Himself our regard for reputation, and if we instinctively shrink from whatever is branded with ignominy and disgrace, how can we imagine that the very fountain of purity shall become corrupt, the very source of honour defiled? The "glory of God" is an expression that contains the most impressive sanction that the imagination of man can conceive. When God plights His glory He plights His right to the love, homage and adoration of His creatures. He plights all claim upon their worship, veneration and obedience. He virtually engages to abdicate His throne and to be stripped of the prerogatives that belong to Him, to lose His own self-respect, to forfeit for ever His name, if He should be found unfaithful to His Word. What a security to the heirs of the promise! How can we hesitate in committing our souls, our interests for time and for eternity, to that everlasting covenant which is charged with the glory of God? What broader foundation could be laid for our faith? As if it were not enough to appeal to us upon the eternal principles of truth and justice and righteousness, as if these were too abstract and impalpable to arouse our sympathies and wake up a warm and living interest, God comes to us in a relation which is pre-eminently personal, and stands before us as one who has a Name to vindicate, and puts His faithfulness on a ground which, in the case of man, a creature like ourselves, we recognize as the most sacred and solemn of all sanctions. As certainly as God cannot deny Himself, as certainly as His own glory is the end of all His works—the scope of every manifestation of His being—as certainly as His own great name is dear to Him, so certainly shall every pledge of His love be redeemed. Not one word of all the good things He hath spoken shall ever fall to the ground. Heaven and earth may pass away, but the Word of the Lord abideth for ever, and this is the Word which by the Gospel is preached unto us. We cannot sufficiently adore that goodness which has stooped to our infirmities, and illustrated this faithfulness by the analogy of principles which address themselves with power to every human heart, and which shut us up to the alternative of faith or the most shocking and abominable imputations upon the Divine character.

I conclude the subject of our engagements with our fellowmen with a caution that cannot be too earnestly inculcated upon the young, and that is—they should never by facility of temper, by reluctance to give offence or anxiety to please, permit themselves to be betrayed into expressions naturally fitted to excite expectations, when it is not their purpose to come under the obligation of a promise. "It must be observed," says Dr. Paley,[1] " that most of those forms of speech which, strictly taken, amount to no more than declarations of present intention, do yet, in the usual way of understanding them, excite the expectation, and therefore carry with them the force, of absolute promises—such as, 'I intend you this place,' 'I design to leave you this estate,' 'I purpose giving you my vote,' 'I mean to serve you;' in which, although the 'intention,' the 'purpose,' the 'design,' the 'meaning' be expressed in words of the present time, yet you cannot afterwards recede from them without a breach of good faith. If you choose, therefore, to make known your present intention, and yet to reserve to yourself the liberty of changing it, you must guard your expressions by an additional clause, as, 'I intend at present,' 'if I do not

[1] Mor. Phil., B. iii., Pt. i., c. 5.

alter,' or the like. And after all, as there can be no reason for communicating your intention but to excite some degree of expectation or other, a wanton change of an intention which is once disclosed always disappoints somebody, and is always for that reason wrong. There is in some men an infirmity with regard to promises which often betrays them into great distress. From the confusion or hesitation or obscurity with which they express themselves, especially when overawed or taken by surprise, they sometimes encourage expectations and bring upon themselves demands which, possibly, they never dreamed of. This is a want not so much of integrity as of presence of mind."

A man's character suffers in the eyes of others, his self-respect is diminished in his own, when he finds himself ensnared into reputed obligations to which he has weakly or foolishly given rise. His ingenuousness and candour are brought under a cloud, and however he may vindicate his name, he cannot but feel that he has put a weapon into the hands of malice. "He that intends," says Jeremy Taylor, "to do himself honour must take care that he be not suspected—that he give no occasion of reproachful language—for fame and honour is a nice thing, tender as a woman's chastity, or like the face of the purest mirror, which a foul breath or an unwholesome air or a watery eye can sully, and the beauty is lost, though it be not dashed in pieces. When a man or a sect is put to answer for themselves in the matter of reputation, they, with their distinctions, wipe the glass, and at last can do nothing but make it appear it was not broken; but their very abstersion and laborious excuses confess it was foul and faulty."

There is but one way of avoiding these painful predicaments, and that is by putting a bridle upon our lips. He that offends not in word is a perfect man. Speech is a sacred prerogative; the tongue rules the word, and we should see to it that our hearts rule it. Let us weigh the import of what we utter, speak with the deliberation of rational and accountable beings, speak according to our real purposes and thoughts, and we shall be saved the mortification and the shame of even an appearance of failure in good faith. It is an awkward thing, and humbling to a good man, to have to defend himself from the imputation of perfidy when malice can give any colour to the charge. As to suspect a servant is to corrupt him, so calumny often drives men to crime. They resent the injustice of mankind by becoming what they have been falsely represented to be. They make reprisals on society by practising the vices of which they have experienced the shame without the guilt. Let us, then, guard with jealous care the sanctity of our faith. Let us avoid even the appearance of evil. Let us even suffer wrong rather than give the least occasion of being suspected of falsehood, duplicity or fraud. If Achilles, who had Chiron for his master, could exult in the ingenuous simplicity of his character, how should he who has had the Son of God for his teacher and example be clothed with truth as with a garment?

The evil of being seduced into engagements contrary to our purpose is not to be compared with that of being ensnared into those that are unlawful. To make a promise or pledge with the consciousness that the matter of it is wrong is a most deliberate compact with the Devil; it is selling one's self to evil. He that does so either intends to keep his word, or he does not. If he intends to keep it, he actually makes evil his good, and approximates as closely as his circumstances will allow to the father of lies, who never speaks truth except when it redeems his engagements to sin. If he does not intend to keep it, he is guilty of deliberate fraud. In either view, the making of an unlawful promise knowingly and voluntarily is an aggravated crime. Few, it is to be hoped, ever reach this pitch of wickedness. But to make an unlawful promise unconsciously is not without sin. It is always rash; and though it is not obligatory, it places a man, when the unlawfulness is discovered, in a very painful situation. It is apt to diminish his sensibility to moral distinctions, to superinduce a sophistry which corrupts the heart and darkens the understanding. The very anxiety to exempt himself from censure will tempt him to prevaricate with duty, and the effort to acquit the criminal may terminate in a justification of the crime. To come in close contact with vice is always dangerous.

> "Seen too oft, familiar with its face,
> We first endure, then pity, then embrace."

To apologize for sin is the next step to the commission of it; and to apologize for it all those will be tempted who have been entangled in unlawful engagements. Let all men, but particularly the young, guard against them with a holy solicitude. Resolve never to make a promise without having well weighed the moral character.of its matter.

Never let a formula implying obligation pass your lips unless you are sure that it relates to nothing which is inconsistent with your duty to God or man. Whatever is not of faith is sin, and he that doubteth is damned. In every undertaking our first care should be to have a clear conscience. Rectitude is a sacred, an awful thing; and as its eternal laws should never be despised by open and deliberate transgression, so the very possibility of invading them by rashness and imprudence should fill us with constant vigilance and unceasing caution. "Ignorance of duty," says Jeremy Taylor, "is always a sin, and therefore, when we are in a perceived discernible state of danger, he that refuses to inquire after his duty does not desire to do it." "We enter upon danger and despise our own safety, and are careless of our duty, and not zealous for God, nor yet subjects of conscience or of the Spirit of God, if we do not well inquire of an action we are to do whether it be good or bad."

To him, however, who has been rashly ensnared I would solemnly say, Do not hesitate to repent of your engagement and to nip the action in the bud. You have sinned already. Do not double the offence by the perpetration of the deed. Let no fear of reproach, no sense of self-degradation, induce you to parley with the crime. You have come too near it already. Your only safety is in instant retreat. If you have betrothed yourself to a harlot under the impression that she was a virgin, flee her poisoned embraces as soon as you find out her pollution. Never, never for an instant think of excusing or extenuating a wrong because you have been implicated in it. The moment you begin to debate you have soiled the purity of your conscience.

DISCOURSE VI.

VOWS.

THERE is a marked difference between Protestant and Romish communions in their estimate of the value and importance of vows as an element of religious worship. The Church of Rome has perverted, and Protestants have neglected, them. The will-worship and superstition fostered by the one have produced a reaction to the opposite extreme in the other. In this, as in most other cases, the truth lies in moderation. It is obvious to remark that this species of devotion has entered into all religions, whether Pagan, Jewish or Christian. Wherever God and Providence have been acknowledged, there, too, have been acknowledged the sanctity of oaths and the piety of vows. A form of worship so universal must be founded in nature, and however it may have been corrupted by the mixture of false doctrines or perverted by ignorance and superstition, there must be something in it which is consistent with reason, and which should be reclaimed from prostitution and restored to its right place among the functions of the religious life. I have no doubt that in the Church of Rome the extravagant commendation of supererogatory works, which are productive of nothing but pain to the flesh and vanity and pride to the spirit, has detracted from the weightier matters of the law, and degraded piety from obedience to God to the punctilious observance of the uncommanded devices of men, while the doctrine of vows in its connection with "a show of wisdom in will-worship and humility, and neglecting of the body," has practically destroyed in many instances all real piety of life. Among Protestants, on the other hand, the general inattention to the principle which has made the vow as universal as the oath has prevented many from apprehending, in anything like their true sacredness and interest, the peculiar obligations of religion. Johnson's horror of a vow is well known. He looked upon it as nothing but a snare to the conscience, and had almost said that he who could not get to heaven without one deserved not to go there at all.

I have thought, therefore, that it would not be amiss to devote a little more attention to this subject than it has usually received from the Protestant pulpit, and have collected my thoughts under the heads of the Nature, Uses and Obligation of Vows.

I. First, then, a vow is of the general nature of a promise. The Schoolmen have discussed the question whether it consists essentially in a mere purpose of the will, or whether the act of reason, which in other instances transmutes a resolution into a promise and gives it its binding force, must here also be superinduced. The definition which confounds it with a deliberate and firm resolution, making it a mere *conceptio boni propositi cum animi deliberatione firmata, qua quis ad aliquid faciendum, vel non faciendum se Deo obligat,* proceeds on the assumption that the only importance of signification in ordinary promises is to make known the thoughts and intent of the heart—that if men could read the purposes of each other as they are secretly formed in the mind, these purposes would instantly create obligations and impart rights. But this is obviously a mistake; there is a broad distinction betwixt a purpose and a promise. The promise is the child of the purpose, but there must be a father to beget it. There must be something added to the purpose before it can bind as an engagement. The intervening act by which a purpose is changed is an ordination of the reason by which the purpose is vol-

untarily made the rule or law of a future thing to be done by
ourselves. The promise sustains the same relation to our
own future acts which a command or order bears to the acts
of a servant. The constituting of this relation is essential to
obligation; it is explicitly enounced by signification in promises among men; it is enough that it exists in promises to
God. This act or ordination of reason is simply the voluntary determination to be considered as bound, *voluntas se
obligandi.* Where this does not obtain either explicitly or
implicitly, a resolution terminates upon ourselves, and carries no other duty along with it than what is essentially
involved in the matter of it. Where it is not signified there
is no promise; where it does not exist, no vow.[1]

2. What distinguishes the vow from every other promise
is the party to whom it is made—God. By virtue of this
relation it becomes an act of religious worship, and partakes
at the same time of the nature of an oath. He takes a very
limited view of what constitutes the worship of God who
restricts it exclusively to those exercises of prayer, praise
or thanksgiving which are specifically religious. Our whole
life should be one great instance of devotion. It is the end,
the intention—or, as the Schoolmen phrase it, the ordination
—of it which determines the character of an act; and if in
all that we do we aim at the glory of God, " every action
of nature becomes religious," every meal an instrument of
piety, every office of ordinary life a holy oblation. It is
the spirit and temper of the soul which settles the question
of worship. A cup of cold water given to a disciple in the
name of a disciple is not simply charity; it is an offering
acceptable to God. As in the vow the ordination of the
action is to God, whatever may be the nature of the thing
to be done, whether natural, civil or spiritual, the action
becomes religious. It takes its denomination from its end.
The writers of the Romish Church make it an act of the
highest religious worship, an act of *latria*, and are accordingly at one with Protestants in affirming that vows can be

---

[1] Aquinas, Summa, 2. 2. Quest. 88, Art. 1.

lawfully made to God only. This, beyond all controversy, is the doctrine of the Scriptures. Hence the indignation of the Lord against the children of Israel for making vows to the queen of heaven. The crime was idolatry.

But a vow is also of the nature of an oath. Although primarily it respects God simply as the party to whom a promise is made, yet secondarily, in consequence of His relations to the creature, it must also regard Him as a witness and a judge. The oath is a solemn invocation of God, in which His name is made the guarantee of the truth of what we say, or, in case of falsehood, in which we deliberately abjure His favour. We suspend our claims to the Divine protection upon our veracity. The peculiarity of its sanction is the reverence for the Divine Being upon which all its sacredness depends. Its peculiar guilt consists in taking the name of the Lord our God in vain. All this is obviously implied in the vow, and hence it may be compendiously defined as a promissory oath, using that phrase, not in its common acceptation as a promise to which men are the parties, confirmed by an oath, but as a promise which is at the same time an oath. The Jews, accordingly, were accustomed to couple imprecations with their vows; the Psalmist repeatedly employs terms of swearing and vowing as synonymous expressions.

3. The circumstance that it is God with whom we have to deal in the vow determines at once the nature of its matter and the spirit or temper in which it should be made. Without entering into the frivolous discussions of the Schoolmen *de bono meliori*, which they made essential to the validity of vows, it is obvious that nothing can legitimately constitute the matter of our engagements which is inconsistent with reverence for His name, forbidden by His Word, hurtful to our virtue, or beyond our strength of nature or of grace. Such oblations, instead of being worship, are a mockery. I would not say (the common doctrine of the schools[1]) that

---

[1] Vota vero quæ sunt de rebus vanis et inutilibus sunt magis deridenda quam servanda. Aquinas, Sum. 2. 2. Quest. 88, Art. 2. Sanderson, in his little treatise *de Juramento*, takes the view which is adopted in the text.

light and frivolous promises, provided they respect things that are not essentially unlawful, are absolutely null : they, no doubt, bind the conscience, but I will say that they argue a contempt of God, and that it is utterly unlawful to make them. To call His awful name upon actions that are silly and ridiculous, that neither in themselves nor their tendencies have a moral significancy, is a crime of impiety and profaneness which is even as the sin of perjury. What can be his conception of God who approaches the terrible Majesty with absurd promises to walk with pebbles in his shoes, to stand for a given time upon a single foot, to lie in a particular posture or to eat with a particular implement, and imagines that these worse than childish follies are accepted as proofs of extraordinary piety ? Verily, their foolish heart is darkened, and they have changed the glory of the incorruptible God into the image of a child, " pleased with a rattle and tickled with a straw."

To guard against profaneness in making vows, let the following cautions in relation to the matter be observed :

(1.) If they respect an act which is specifically religious, which is directly and immediately, and not merely by virtue of the intention, an act of worship, let it be well settled that it is appointed in the Word of God. As it is the prerogative of the monarch to ordain the ceremonial of his court, so it belongs exclusively to God to determine by what external observances His holy name shall be honoured. Nothing is more offensive or insulting than will-worship. He takes such pleasure in obedience " that He pronounces a curse," says Calvin,[1] " on all acts of will-worship, however specious and splendid they may be in the eyes of men. If God abominates all voluntary services invented by us without His command, it follows that nothing can be acceptable to Him except what is appointed by His Word. Let us not, therefore, assume to ourselves such a great liberty as to presume to vow to God anything that has no testimony of His

[1] Institutes, Book iv., chap. 13.

approbation." In vain do they worship Me, teaching for doctrines the commandments of men.

(2.) In the next place, if the vow respects any other act, let us be certain that the act is either the elicit or imperate one of some virtue—that is, that it consists in doing something positively commanded or avoiding something positively forbidden, or in making that which is naturally indifferent conduce to our improvement. There can be no doubt about the lawfulness of engagements to perform our duty or to abstain from sin. All elicit acts of virtue are clearly within the scope of a vow. But the case is not as plain when it comes to the curtailment of Christian liberty. That should not be done except to save ourselves from temptation or others from offence. When an indifferent thing, by being specially sanctified to God, can promote my own piety or the piety of others, it seems to me that it can legitimately constitute the matter of a vow. Liberty is then used for the glory of God, and the use of it is manifestly consistent with His will. In the language of the schools, it becomes a greater good. This is the doctrine of Thomas Aquinas.[1] "Maceration of one's own body," says he, "by vigils and fasts, for example, is not accepted of God, except in so far as it is a work of virtue—that is, in so far as it is done with proper discretion for the purpose of restraining concupiscence without too much inconvenience to nature." The same is the doctrine of Calvin. "If a person," says he, "has fallen into any crime through the vice of intemperance, nothing prevents him from correcting that vice by a temporary renunciation of all delicacies, and enforcing this abstinence by a vow to lay himself under the stronger obligation." "Yet," he adds, "I impose no perpetual law on those who have been guilty of such an offence: I only point out what they are at liberty to do if they think that such a vow would be useful to them. I consider a vow of this kind, therefore, as

---

[1] Summa, 2. 2. Quest. 88, Art. 2. See, also, Bishop Hall, Cases of Conscience, Decade iii., case 4. Bishop Reynolds on Hosea.

lawful, but at the same time left to the free choice of every individual."

(3.) The matter of a vow should, further, be something clearly in our own power, either according to the strength of nature or the promises of grace. In the case of commanded duties or prohibited sins we can throw ourselves upon the everlasting covenant, and should make all our engagements in humble reliance upon its provisions. But in uncommanded instances we should measure our ability before we venture to assume so solemn an obligation. The aids of grace will be imparted only in so far as may be conducive to God's glory; and as the circumstances which to-day justify a particular use of liberty may change to-morrow, no man can contract any permanent obligations in regard to these things in dependence upon God's help. He has no promise to justify such faith. Vows of this class, therefore, should always be temporary; otherwise they become a temptation and a snare. To illustrate my meaning: there may be a conjuncture of circumstances which render it highly inexpedient at one time for a man to marry. It may subsequently, by a change in his condition, be as evidently his duty to do so. If, now, he had contracted a vow of perpetual celibacy, he has engaged to do what he is not sure that he shall have strength to perform, and what God has nowhere promised to enable him to do. The Lord has commanded chastity, and all His people may rely upon His grace to preserve them from uncleanness. But chastity is not virginity; the wife is as pure as the virgin, the husband as chaste as the eunuch. We dare not, therefore, pledge ourselves to perpetual continence when it may be that God designs to protect our purity by the holy estate of wedlock. This is the class of vows which entangle the conscience— those which relate to matters of indifference, that only partake of the character of virtue in the way of accident. Hence the advice of Taylor, "Let not young beginners in religion enlarge their hearts and straiten their liberty by vows of long continuance; nor indeed can any one else without a great experience of himself and of all accidental dangers. Vows of single actions are safest, and proportionable to those single blessings ever begged in such cases of sudden and transient importunities."

The matter of one class of vows is the consecration of a person or thing to the service and glory of God. The thing to be done is the renunciation of all rights of property on our part and the devotion of the object, whatever it may be, to the service and glory of God. Such was Hannah's vow: " And she vowed a vow and said, O Lord of Hosts, if Thou wilt indeed look on the affliction of Thine handmaid, and remember me and not forget Thine handmaid, and will give unto Thine handmaid a man-child, then will I give him unto the Lord all the days of his life, and there shall no razor come upon his head." Such also was Jacob's vow—he consecrated the stone and the tithes to the Lord: " And Jacob vowed a vow, saying, if God will be with me and keep me in the way that I go, and will give me bread to eat and raiment to put on, so that I come again to my father's house in peace, then shall the Lord be my God, and this stone which I have set for a pillar shall be God's house, and of all that Thou shalt give me I will surely give the tenth unto Thee." These are what Calvin calls vows of thanksgiving. He finds " other examples of them in the ancient peace-offerings, which used to be vowed by pious kings and generals entering on just wars, to be offered in case they should obtain the victory, or by persons labouring under more than common difficulties in case the Lord would deliver them. Thus we are to understand all those places in the Psalms which speak of vows. Vows of this kind may also be now used among us whenever God delivers us from any great calamity, from a severe disease or from any other danger. For on such occasions it is not inconsistent with the duty of a pious man to consecrate to God some oblation that he has vowed, merely as a solemn token of grateful acknowledgment, that he may not appear unthankful for his goodness." Such, it may be added, is the vow implied in the very nature of the Christian profession. A man yields himself to God a living sacrifice; he is sanctified to the Divine service and glory, renounces all right of property in himself, and dedicates his faculties and members as instruments of righteousness unto holiness. Such also is a good man's consecration of his children to the Lord; they are devoted, and he feels that he has no more right to train them for merely secular ends than an ancient Jew had to use the vessels of the sanctuary for the ordinary purposes of life. It is nothing less than sacrilege to treat them in any other way than as holy to the Lord. The vow of personal consecration made in baptism is repeated in every reception of the Lord's Supper. The sacraments are seals of a covenant by which God certifies His promises to us, and by which we solemnly pledge an absolute allegiance to Him. Every Christian man, therefore, can justly appropriate the language of David with all the comfort and consolation it imparts: "Thy vows are upon me, O God;" and with the Apostle he rejoices that he is not his own, but is bought with a price.

II. Having sufficiently indicated the nature of vows, I proceed to the question of their use. Is it or is it not expedient to make them? Of course the discussion must be confined to those which are lawful and proper, which are consistent with the will of God, not rashly made nor disproportioned to our powers.

There is but little force in the objections, in so far as such vows are concerned, that they curtail our liberty, multiply temptations and are without warrant from the example of Christ and His Apostles. There is no abridgment of liberty in strengthening the bonds of duty, no necessary peril in what nothing but depravity can convert into an instrument of sin, and no reflection upon Christ, whose whole life was a vow, nor upon the Apostles, who were body and soul devoted to the work of the Lord. That is not freedom which absolves from obligation, that is not a snare which is only made so by our voluntary neglect, and that is not unchristian which aims at the perfection of Christian life. The truth is, the whole question concerning the utility of vows turns upon the spirit and temper in which they are made. They have no absolute efficacy in themselves; there is no charm by which the mere making of them shall be an instrument of good. All depends upon the state of mind which prompts them, the purpose and ends for which they are made. Here, as in everything else, the maxim of the Apostle holds good: Whatsoever is not of faith is sin.

1. If vows are made in the spirit of bribes, if they proceed from low and degrading thoughts of the Godhead, and are presented as inducements which have an intrinsic value in the court of Heaven, they are insults to Deity and injuries to us. God maintains no intercourse of barter and traffic with His creatures, and those who look upon His covenants as the interchange of reciprocal benefits are puffed up with pride, and have already fallen into the condemnation of the Devil. All things come of Him, and it is only of His own that we can give Him.

2. In the next place, those who look upon vows as instances of extraordinary merit eviscerate them of all their tendencies to good. There is no righteousness but in obedience to God, and as the vow is only an acknowledgment of duty, coupled with a fixed resolution to perform it, there is nothing more in it than the honesty of a debtor who admits the debt and makes arrangements to discharge it. So far are those vows which respect uncommanded instances from possessing extraordinary merit that the sole merit or moral excellence which belongs to them is derivative and secondary; it springs from their relation to commanded duties. They are the merest puerilities except as they are ordained to the ends of virtue. They become lawful only when they are assumed as the instruments or means of enforcing prime obligations. They are like the ancient phylacteries, memorials of duty rather than duties themselves. To treat them, therefore, as proofs of extraordinary righteousness is to reverse the relation of means and end, and to substitute

the sign for the thing signified. He that enters into engagements of this sort, with the secret feeling that he is pleasing the Lord of hosts with the display of unwonted zeal, may expect the confounding rebuke that "obedience is better than sacrifice, and to hearken than the fat of rams." It is the preposterous notion that there is something more than God requires, a righteousness of supererogation, in these instances of vows, that has corrupted the whole subject and made it stink in the nostrils of humble piety. This dead fly has polluted the whole box of ointment. The Divine law is the standard of moral perfection, and nothing is good which does not express the spirit and temper of this perfect standard. There is no going beyond it; there may be a fearful falling short of it. Whatever expedients we employ to impress this law upon the conscience and to engrave it in the very texture of the will, they are good or otherwise according to their tendencies to secure the result. The man is righteous or unrighteous, holy or sinful, according as his heart is in union and sympathy with the holy commandment. The effect of exalting supererogatory observances above simple obedience, and treating him pre-eminently as a saint, whatever may be the general temper and disposition of his mind, who excels in ascetic devotions, has been to degrade religion from its noble eminence as a reasonable service to the emptiest show of fooleries. Vows conceived in such a spirit are as fatal to prosperity as the mildew or pestilence. They are a high conspiracy against heaven, an impious and daring attempt to reverse the order which God has established, and to make His will subordinate and secondary to the little contrivances of man. It is to subvert morality and to convert religion into superstition. Hence Taylor, in his Holy Living, in order to obviate this tendency to pervert the vow into will-worship, has very reasonably advised, "that every vow of a new action be also accompanied with a new degree and enforcement of our essential and unalterable duty. Such was Jacob's vow, that (besides the payment of a tithe) God should be his

God, that so he might strengthen his duty to Him, first in essentials and precepts, and then in additionals and accidentals. For it is but an ill tree that spends more in leaves and suckers and gums than in fruit, and that thankfulness and religion is best that first secures duty and then enlarges in counsels."

3. Vows that are made in conformity with the spirit of the Gospel, with proper views of the majesty and goodness of God and of the weakness and ill-desert of man, made in faith and as the honest expressions of sincere worship, are undoubted helps to piety. These are not the vows which become hindrances and snares.

(1.) In the first place, they obviously strengthen the general bonds of duty. They consecrate the offices of life. They diffuse the influence and savour of the Divine name around moral and civil observances, and attach the sacredness of religion to everything which they touch. The vow introduces a new sanction, and the sanction which of all others is dearest to the Christian heart—reverence for the glory of God. It pronounces the Divine name, and makes that to be specifically religious which before was only natural or civil, and thus superinduces what Augustin calls a " blessed necessity to good." It confirms the will by a direct sense of the majesty and holiness of God. It is, indeed, the general spirit of religion concentrated on a single act. As the peculiar motive of the vow is reverence for God, it is manifest that every instance of fidelity strengthens the principle until it is matured into the stability of habit.

(2.) In the next place, vows are conducive to piety by increasing the sense of union with God. They keep alive the consciousness that we are His and that He is ours. David, when overwhelmed by afflictions and oppressed by dangers, often established his heart with the reflection that the vows of his God were upon him. The feeling was, that God had a peculiar interest in him as one devoted to His service, and that the Deity was not likely to abandon His own property as a spoil to men of violence and blood. We keep aloof from the Throne of grace when we distrust our right to be found there; nearness of access is in proportion to the feeling of intimacy betwixt God and the creature. It is precisely this feeling which the vow cherishes. This is eminently the case with that general vow of consecration which is involved in the very notion of the Christian profession; its language is, My beloved is mine and I am His. We know that God careth for His own; and in proportion as we cherish the conviction that we belong to Him, will be the frequency of our approaches to His seat and the strength of our reliance on His name. It is the prerogative of faith to appropriate God and the promises of the covenant; and whatever has a tendency to increase the feeling of propriety reacts upon faith, and strengthens that very feature of it by which it is made the instrument at once of comfort and of growth in grace. There is no privilege, no exaltation of blessedness, comparable with that by which a sinner is permitted to avouch the Lord to be his God. Everything of good, whether for this world or that which is to come, is embraced in the compendious declaration, I will be a God to thee and to thy seed after thee. The vow corresponds to this promise, and presents the man as an oblation to the Lord, holy and acceptable through Jesus Christ. It is an exercise of faith which strengthens faith.

(3.) In the third place, vows in exercising specific virtues contribute to the habit of them, and, through the intimate connection which obtains among them, fortify the general principle of integrity. Calvin recognizes four ends to which our vows may be rightly directed—two referring to the past and two to the future. "To the time past belong those vows by which we either testify our gratitude to God for benefits received, or, in order to deprecate His wrath, inflict punishment upon ourselves for sins we have committed. The former may be called vows of thanksgiving; the latter, vows of penitence." The vows which he refers to the future " have for their object, partly to render us more cautious of danger, partly to stimulate us to the performance of duty."

It cannot be denied that whatever strengthens the sentiment of gratitude, or reminds us of our own guilt and unworthiness, whatever guards us against future temptations or arms us for future conflict, is of no mean utility to the Divine life. The stronger the tie which binds us to God and duty the better. If a man honestly aims at the Divine glory and his own spiritual improvement, if his heart is right, the solemn bonds of a vow will co-operate mightily with the ordinary sanctions of law. The precept binds by its native force; the obligation is sweetened when a man chooses it by a free act and rewrites it upon his conscience. The vow becomes an additional security for obedience, and every instance of fidelity is an instance of moral progress. To the conscientious man a vow is a monitor, a heavenly mentor constantly at his side, and when the flesh would plead and remonstrate, it gently whispers, " Remember that this duty has been made your choice. Your vow did not create the obligation, although in uncommanded instances it gave a specific consent, but, already existing, your vow accepted it, and accepted it as a good."

The truth is, all the objections that can be justly urged against the benefit of vows apply only to that class of them which are rash and imprudent—which are either offensive in matter or relate to acts which we have no warrant for assuming an obligation to perform.

Still, I am far from thinking that vows should be made common. To make them common is to cheapen them, to reduce them to the level of ordinary obligations; and when this process is once begun, the next step will be to deny the reality of all obligations which have not been self-imposed. Human nature is a weak thing; and as its tendency is to run into extremes, it would be nothing strange that it should oscillate from the point of highest reverence for a vow to that of comparative contempt. What I insist on is, that the vow is an act of solemn religious worship; that it is of the nature of an oath; and that, when properly used for proper ends and on proper occasions, it is eminently conducive to virtue. It loses its efficacy, however, just as the oath does, if made the ordinary form of Christian obedience. It should be reserved for extraordinary occasions, when we wish to erect a monument to God's goodness or a memorial of our own shame, or to begin a new epoch in the Christian life. Familiarity here, as in the case of the oath, is destructive of reverence. There is a marked difference between the questions whether the vow, as an extraordinary act of worship—that is, in its true character and relations—or as an ordinary act of worship—that is, perverted from its true character and relations—is of beneficial tendency. No one can be more deeply sensible than I am that the consequences of the habit of turning every duty into a vow are pernicious in the extreme. It proceeds from a weak and superstitious spirit, and if permitted to operate without check will multiply scruples until it converts religion into torture. The abuse of vows consists in their frequency. Let that be guarded against, and they can certainly be turned to a good account. The occasions on which they should be resorted to every man must determine for himself. His own heart is the best expositor of extraordinary circumstances in his own life. He knows its critical points, the events which have given shape and direction to his history and have left their mark upon his character.

III. The next point to be discussed is the obligation of vows. The fact of their obligation is, of course, not disputed. The convictions of every heart coincide here with the positive declarations of Scripture: "When thou shalt vow a vow unto the Lord thy God, thou shalt not slack to pay it, for the Lord thy God will surely require it of thee; and it would be sin in thee. That which is gone out of thy lips, thou shalt keep and perform: even a free-will offering, according as thou hast vowed unto the Lord thy God, which thou hast promised with thy mouth." "When thou vowest a vow unto God, defer not to pay it, for He hath no pleasure in fools: pay that which thou hast vowed. Better is it that thou shouldest not vow, than that thou shouldest vow and

not pay." "Vow and pay unto the Lord your God." But
while the fact is clear, the immediate grounds of the obligation are not directly stated, though they are implicitly
assumed.

I cannot forbear to notice how completely the theory of
Dr. Paley in regard to the obligation of promises breaks
down in its application to vows. He is perfectly conscious
of it, and frankly confesses it, and yet it seems to have
raised no sort of misgivings as to the soundness of his principles. It is clear that whatever is the formal cause of the
obligation of a promise as such must extend to every promise; the whole essence must be found in the species. The
production of a case, therefore, in which a promise really
exists, and yet is not binding upon the given ground, is conclusive evidence that the ground in question is not the formal
cause of obligation in any promise. *Falsus in uno, falsus in
omnibus.* We are shut up to the admission either that there
is no specific reason in the case, or that Dr. Paley's theory
is false—either no promise is obligatory because it is a
promise, or Dr. Paley has failed to indicate why any is
obligatory. Listen to his naïve confession: "Vows are
promises to God. The obligation cannot be made out upon
the same principle as that of other promises. The violation
of them, nevertheless, implies a want of reverence to the
Supreme Being; which is enough to make it sinful." Vows
are promises, but they do not oblige because they are promises. There can be no deception in the case, and consequently no breach of confidence reposed, which makes it so
important to keep other promises. But though not binding
as promises, they are still to be kept, because a breach of
them implies a want of reverence for the Supreme Being.
But how does this want of reverence appear? If there was
nothing sacred in the vow considered as a promise, if it
carried no obligation or enjoined no duty, if it were a mere
moral nullity, where is the want of reverence to be found?
Did not Dr. Paley feel in penning, and does not every reader
feel in perusing, these lines, that it is precisely because the

vow is binding as a promise that the violation of it casts contempt upon God. Such inconsistencies and contradictions result from partial schemes of philosophy ; and this is one, among the thousand that might be produced, which convicts the system of "expediency," as expounded by Dr. Paley, of gross and flagrant falsehood. Of all philosophies it is the most shallow and superficial, and its principal recommendation is to simple minds, whom it flatters with the belief that they are possessed of principles, without the labour of patient thought.

The true ground of the obligation of vows is very easily explained. We have but to recur to the definition—a promise made to God, or a promise which is, at the same time, an oath. As a promise it is obligatory from the twofold consideration of truth and justice which has been already explained. God is a person, and we may maintain relations to Him analogous to those which subsist among men. We can give Him of His own. The notion is preposterous that our engagements to the Almighty do not give Him a covenanted right to exact obedience at our hands. He does not deal with us as things. In making us originally in His own glorious image He stamped it upon us as the prerogative of our nature to be persons, and in conformity with this high distinction He conducts all the dispensations of His providence towards us. We are always treated by Him as persons. We are not tools and instruments, but conscious and responsible agents, capable of giving and receiving rights. Hence the relation of justice, pre-eminently a personal relation in our intercourse with Him as well as with one another. And although the cattle upon a thousand hills are His, and He has no need of our sacrifices and offerings—though we ourselves belong to Him, and all that we have and are—yet He condescends to accept at our hands what is our own by a free donation from Himself. He permits us to transfer to Him such rights as we have, and even represents Himself, all blessed though He be, as injured by faithless dealings on our part. Hence the Scriptures do not hesitate to speak of

Him as wronged, robbed, defrauded. The very passages
which inculcate the faithful observance of a vow put it distinctly on the ground of justice—it is the payment of a debt.
If Dr. Paley had apprehended the essential rectitude of truth
and justice, he would have seen the folly of resolving the
obligation of promises into the inconveniences of deceit, and
would have been saved his embarrassment in the awkward
effort to make infidelity to God a sin.   A rustic could have
told him, "I must fulfil my vow, because my word is out,
and God has a right to expect it of me."

But a vow also partakes of the nature of an oath ; this
is its specific difference.   And while it binds as a promise
upon the grounds of truth and justice, it binds as an oath
upon the principle of reverence for God.   He that keeps a
vow is not only just, but pious ; he that breaks it is not only
guilty of injustice, but perjury.   Hence the enormous malignity of the sin.   The Word of God, as well as the common
consent of all civilized nations, has attributed the highest
degree of sanctity to the oath, and he that is not held by it
has cut loose from all moral obligations.   He that has no
reverence for the awful name of God has severed the last tie
which binds him to truth.   He is an outlaw in the universe,
a star of disastrous omen that has broken beyond the attrac-
tion of its central sun, and must be left to pursue its course
unchecked by the only power that could keep it in its orbit.
Nullum vinculum ad astringendam fidem, says Cicero, *majores
nostri jure-jurando arctius esse voluerunt.*   And the highest
authority has assured us that the Lord will not hold him
guiltless that taketh His name in vain.   So sacred were
oaths esteemed among the ancient Romans that they needed
no protection from law.   The perjured man was simply
exposed by the censor, and that was enough.   The brand
of infamy was upon him, and like the taint of leprosy
debarred him from the fellowship of his species and left
him to the vengeance of the insulted god.

And yet what gives to perjury its malignity above a common lie—and it is a thought which I would earnestly im-

press upon the youthful mind—is perhaps the most common of all the sins that are daily committed; it is want of reverence for God. The oath or vow-breaker carries it to the point of positive contempt. He openly defies that august and terrible Majesty before which angels bow and the archangel veils his face. It is a sin, the enormity of which the imagination cannot conceive, because no thought can compass the infinite excellence of Him whose prerogative it is to be, who sits upon the circle of the earth, and the inhabitants thereof are as grasshoppers, who stretcheth out the heavens as a curtain and spreadeth them out as a tent to dwell in. That a puny creature of the dust, born to-day and gone to-morrow, should have the audacity to pour contempt upon that glorious Name which seraphs adore with rapture is enough to astonish the heavens and convulse the earth. Yea, still more astonishing is that miracle of patience which endures the monsters, when one word would arm all nature against them, make the ground treacherous beneath them, heaven terrible above them and hell ready to meet them at their coming. The magnitude of the sin cannot be exaggerated, and yet the principle to which it is indebted for its pre-eminence in guilt is constantly exemplified in the speech and intercourse of those who would be shocked at the imputation of anything that approximates to perjury. Profane swearing, light and frivolous appeals to the Almighty, the indiscriminate use of the lot—all these are only different forms of expressing irreverence for God. They contain the ingredients of the same poison with perjury and vow-breach. It is a startling reflection that the very circumstance which distinguishes these from an ordinary falsehood, and has armed the sentiments of mankind against them, brands the speech of the profane swearer with the same species of crime. It is not, I admit, the same in degree, but it is the same in kind. The thoughtlessness which is often pleaded in extenuation of the guilt is a confession of the fact. It is a proof how little veneration the name of God inspires when we can pronounce it in reiterated blasphemies without even being conscious that a word is escaping from our lips which fills all heaven with awe. It is a proof how near we come to despising it when we can use it in the mere wantonness of sport as a convenient expletive to fill up the chasms of discourse. It is a proof that all respect for it is gone when we can use it to point a jest, to season obscenity and to garnish a tale. It is enough to make the blood curdle to think of the name of God bandied about as a bauble and plaything of fools. This offence cannot go unpunished. If there be a God, He must vindicate His own majesty and glory. There must be a period when all shall tremble before Him, when every knee shall bow and every heart shall do reverence. The sword of justice cannot always be sheathed, nor the arm of vengeance slumber. Engrave it upon your minds, fix it in the very depths of your souls, that it is a fearful thing to make light of God. It is the very spirit and essence of all evil, the very core of iniquity. There is no language of earnestness in which I would not warn you against it, no language of expostulation or entreaty in which I would not implore you against it. If you could see it as the angels see it, or as the spirits of just men made perfect see it; if you could see it as you yourselves will see it in that day when God shall arise to shake terribly the earth, when Jesus shall sit upon the throne of His glory, and the tribes of earth shall be gathered before Him; if you could see it as it is, in the naked enormity of its guilt,— you would flee from it as from the very pestilence of death. You may sport with the whirlwind and trifle with the storm, you may lay your hand upon the lion's mane and play with the leopard's spots, you may go to the very crater of a burning volcano and laugh at the lava which it belches out in thunder, you may trifle with any and everything, but trifle not with God. Let there be one holy thing upon which you dare not lay a profane hand, and let that be the Name of God. Above all things let His throne be sacred and His praise be glorious. Who would not fear Thee, O Thou King of saints?

There are reflections suggested by this subject which, at the risk of being tedious, I cannot repress. In treating of the benefit of vows I had occasion to allude to the comfort and strength imparted to the true believer by the consciousness that he belongs to God. This thought is an anchor to the soul amid the storms of temptation and adversity; it carries assurance of Divine care and of Divine protection. But it has its counterpart; and though the everlasting covenant is so ordered that the Lord will never depart from His children to do them good, yet this very kindness towards them aggravates the crime of their unfaithfulness to Him. It is mournful to reflect to what a fearful extent spiritual perjury obtains. The vows of God are upon us, we profess to be devoted to Him, and yet our pledges are unredeemed, our promises forgotten, our faith broken. He has taken us into a covenant which keeps us, and yet we live for the world; we forget His glory in our pleasures and our gains. The mark cannot be discerned upon our foreheads, and through us His precious Name is profaned. The most faithful have occasion to blush, the daughter of Zion may well bow her head in the dust. If God tenderly forgives us, surely we can never forgive ourselves for the ingratitude, the meanness, the baseness of not keeping faith with Him who is the very fountain and source of truth.

But you congratulate yourselves, perhaps, that you are exempt from the temptation to spiritual perjury. The vows of God are not upon you. You have entered into no engagements to serve Him, and consequently, whatever other crimes you may commit, you are free from the charge of breaking faith with your Maker. There is in this condition no cause of exultation. The exemption from one specific sin is purchased at a dreadful price. You are, according to the statement, aliens from the commonwealth of Israel and strangers to the covenants of promise. You are without Christ, and consequently without God and without hope in the world. There is something overwhelming in the thought of having no God to go to, and yet this is the

condition, and the only condition, upon which you can plead
immunity from the possibility of breaking vows.

But is it certain that the vows of God are not on you?
It may be that your parents at your birth solemnly devoted
you to Him. This act of theirs, sanctioned by His authority, you are bound to respect, and all the engagements in
regard to you, which consistently with parental rights they
have made, you are bound to observe. They were your
guardians before you were conscious of the need of a pro-
tector, and if they have devoted you to God, you are not at
liberty to regard yourselves as your own. You cannot without sacrilege prostitute your talents, faculties and members
to a profane purpose. Holiness to the Lord must be written
upon your foreheads, and when you forget the obligations
it implies, and walk in the light of your own eyes and after
the imaginations of your own hearts, you as much despise the
covenanted claims of God as if you had given yourselves to
His service by your own free act. You have been made a
vessel of the sanctuary; and in surrendering your being to
secular ends you are guilty of the same species of sin which
he commits who defiles the temple of the Lord. Think
not, therefore, to escape the guilt of profaneness by pleading
the absence of vows. It was Solomon who built and consecrated the august edifice on Moriah, but, being consecrated,
it was sacred to all generations. I am afraid that the sanctity of the relation which the piety of the parents has con-
stituted between their children and God is very inadequately
understood. The young do not recognize and feel the right
which it gives Him to them; they do not appreciate their
state of external holiness, and consequently fail to comprehend the malignity of guilt which is involved in the absence
of inward purity. It is a great blessing to be thus in covenant with God; it is an equal curse to despise it. I beseech
you, therefore, to bethink yourselves, and while you are
boasting that you are free from perjury take care that you
are not tainted with sacrilege. It is the same sin, profaneness, in a different dress.

But is it so that you are free from vows which you have voluntarily assumed? Do you not remember the time when your days were consumed like smoke, and your bones burned as an hearth, when your souls abhorred all manner of meat, and you drew near to the gates of death? Do you not remember your anxious thoughts, your solemn reflections, your agonizing fears? Then you cried unto the Lord in your trouble, and in the depths of your distress bound yourselves to His service. Have you forgotten the promise you made when you trembled at the mouth of the grave? Have you forgotten the vows which you uttered when you shrunk in terror from the prospect of eternity? "When He slew them, then they sought Him, and they returned and inquired early after God. And they remembered that God was their Rock, and the high God their Redeemer."[1] These vows, be assured, are recorded in heaven; they imposed a solemn obligation on your souls, from which no power on earth can release you; and if unredeemed they will confront and haunt you in the day of retribution and throughout eternity as the ghosts of the murdered. Such flattering with the mouth, such lying with the tongue when the heart is not right with God nor steadfast in His covenant, such promises made to procure favours and forgotten as soon as the favours are enjoyed, are a mixture of ingratitude, perfidy and profaneness which cannot escape vengeance. Talk not of your exemption from perjury when such witnesses are prepared to testify against you. Wipe not your mouths, and carelessly protest that you have done nothing wrong, when you have lied unto God and proved recreant to the most solemn engagements that it is possible for man to make. You are perjured, your souls are blackened with guilt, and unless they are purged and washed through the blood of the everlasting covenant, it will be like a mill-stone around your necks to sink you to the lowest hell. God is not to be mocked. The conduct which in relation to a fellow-man would doom you to infamy—think you it loses

[1] Ps. lxxviii. 34, 35.

any of its atrocity when directed to Him who is the very
centre and perfection of right? The greatest and best of
beings, is He alone to be degraded so low in the scale of
personal existence that faith and honour lose their significancy when applied to our intercourse with Him? Tell it
not in Gath, publish it not in the streets of Askelon!

There are other occasions on which you have remembered
God and solemnly plighted your faith that you would serve
Him. When the pestilence was walking in darkness and
destruction wasting at noonday, when a thousand were falling at your side and ten thousand at your right hand, when
you were afraid of the terror by night and the arrow that
flieth by day, then you sought the protection of the Almighty
with promises and vows, with strong crying and tears. You
are a father, and have you forgotten the resolutions which
you bound upon your soul as you hung over the form of a
dying child or consigned its dead body to the grave? You
are a husband, and do you not remember the agony of your
prayers when you implored the Almighty to spare the wife
of your bosom? Have you forgotten the promises, thrice
repeated, by which you hoped to redeem your beloved one
from the jaws of death? She still lives, but where are
those vows?

You are thoughtless and impenitent. There was a time
when you trembled at the Word of God—when the sense of
guilt was fastened upon your consciences, and your bones
waxed old through your roaring all the day long. You felt
that you were a sinner and must be born again. But you
were not yet ready for the change. Did you not, in the
conflicts of your spirit, solemnly pledge yourselves to God,
that at a given time, when a given scheme was accomplished,
you would turn to Him and live? That time has come and
gone, that scheme has been realized, but where are you?

It is vain for any man who has a conscience, and who believes in Providence and law, it is vain for any man who
has ever reflected upon his nature and his prospects, to
allege that he is under no vows to God. We have all made

them, and, alas! we have all broken them. Their wrecks may be seen along the whole course of our history; perfidy and ingratitude have marked our career; our lives have been a vast, unbroken lie, and our true posture is with our hands on our mouths and our faces in the dust. When I reflect upon the magnitude of human guilt in this single aspect of it, I am amazed and confounded at the long-suffering forbearance of God. Antecedently to experience no creature could have dreamed that Infinite Holiness could have endured for a day or an hour such monsters of ingratitude, treachery and fraud as we have shown ourselves to be in the whole course of our dealings with the Father of lights. I am ashamed of myself, I am ashamed of my species, when I recollect how false and faithless we have been. Who can boast of his honour, who can scorn the imputation of a lie, when there are promises in heaven unredeemed, vows that are forgotten or despised? Who dares glory in his righteousness when the first principles of justice are openly transgressed? No, no. We have all sinned and come short of the glory of God. But in His amazing goodness there is a remedy. All-guilty as we are, we can be pardoned and accepted; all-polluted as we are, we can be purified and cleansed. There is a fountain opened in the house of David for sin and uncleanness. Let us wash in that fountain, and we shall come forth new men—men of real truth, honour and integrity. The laws of God will be put into our minds and written upon our hearts, and the Spirit of all grace will effectually train us for glory, honour and immortality, and crown us with eternal life. "Oh that men would praise the Lord for His goodness and for His wonderful works to the children of men!"

DISCOURSE VII.

CONSISTENCY.

THE primary notion of consistency, according to the etymology of the word, is that of the agreement or correspondence, the *standing together*, of things compared, and it receives different names according to the cause or effects of the agreement in question. When the things compared are our life and opinions at successive periods of our history, there emerges the meaning of constancy or firmness, the man—the cause of the coincidence—being felt to have stood his ground. When the things compared are our conduct and relations, the agreement or proportion is denominated decency—the effect produced upon the mind of the spectator. When the relations are moral, the deportment which corresponds to them is virtue; when external and incidental, the deportment is simply decorum. When the things compared are our professions and our deeds, we receive the commendation of sincerity or faithfulness, according to the nature of the professions themselves. The man's principles and life stand harmoniously together. Hence, by an easy and natural application of its primary import, consistency embraces stability of opinion, harmony of life and decency or propriety of behaviour, including equally the obligations of rectitude and the lesser morality of manners. It is only in the sense of constancy that it is properly referred to the department of truth, as in that sense it indicates honesty of sentiment, and fulfils the expectations which our principles, character and conduct—a species of promise—have excited. Though it is essential to integrity, the necessary result of truth in the inward parts, yet in itself considered constancy is neither a virtue nor a vice. Its moral character depends upon the moral character of the past, which it continues to reproduce and to perpetuate. It expresses only the notion of perseverance or continuance; it transmits the man unchanged from one period of his being to another, and as there may be uniformity in wickedness as well as steadfastness in duty, consistency is entitled to praise or blame, not for itself, but according to the nature of the things in which it pursues the even tenor of its way. There is no credit in perseverance unless it be a perseverance in right. When our professions and conduct give a promise of sin, we are no more at liberty to gratify the expectations they excite than to keep any other unlawful engagement. Repentance, or a radical change of mind, a thorough revolution of purpose and of life, is as much a duty as to be steadfast and unmovable when our previous course has abounded in the work of the Lord. To persevere is a virtue only when we have begun well. When the past has been right, then, and then only, should the future be shaped in conformity with it. Consistency in this case is nothing but the continued recognition of the supremacy of right, the predominance in every successive moment of our history of the unchanging obligations of morality and religion. The obligation of it is only another name for the unceasing obligation of virtue. We are to be uniform and constant in well-doing, because the same reason which requires integrity to-day will exact it tomorrow; the same reason which requires us to begin requires us to hold on. The succession of moments or the revolution of years makes no change in the stable principles of rectitude. They, like their Eternal Author, are without variableness or shadow of turning—the same yesterday, to-day and for ever. As long as the elements of moral responsibility attach to us, whether our winters have been few or many, the same rules

of truth, justice, piety and benevolence must continue to
regulate our lives. Duty is determined by our nature and
not by our age. Increasing years, it is true, unfold new
relations and develop larger capacities. The circle of
duty may expand, but its nature is subject to no change.
With this preliminary explanation I proceed to the consideration of the general subject of consistency as embraced
under the head of constancy—the only one which falls
within the scope of these discourses, including stability of
opinion and harmony of life.

I. Stability of opinion, it deserves to be remarked, is—

1. Not incompatible with all change. Absolute immutability is the prerogative of God alone. It would not be a
perfection even in Him were He not perfect in all other
respects, so that the notion of change involves necessarily
the notion of deterioration or injury. Finite creatures, from
the very law of their nature, are subject to change in being
made capable of improvement. Their growth, expansion
and development of faculties, the invigoration of their
habits and confirmation of their principles, are all so many
changes for the better. To exempt them from change would
be to stereotype their imbecility and ignorance. When we
commend consistency of opinion we neither mean to exclude
progress nor the abandonment of error. If through the
operation of any cause a man has adopted as true what he
subsequently finds to be false, genuine consistency requires
that he should relinquish the dogma. The pervading love
of truth is the spirit which should regulate all of our opinions, the standard by which consistency is to be tried, the
touchstone of intellectual integrity. Whatever doctrines or
sentiments are not the results of its operation are prejudices,
even should they chance not to be errors, and whatever
changes are effected through its energy and influence are
elements of progress, and contribute to the real perfection
of our nature. He only deserves the commendation of
firmness of opinion who begins with the predominating love
of truth, and maintains it steadily and sincerely in all the

subsequent periods of his history. The law of his intellect-ual life gives unity and consistency to all the operations of his mind. Amid all his changes he has still been the same. The streamlet winds around rocks and hills, but it still bends its course to the river as the river bends its course to the sea. The uniform ascendency of candour, or the love of truth, is the life and soul of the only species of consist-ency which a wise man desires to possess. To have an opinion to-day merely because we had it yesterday, without reference to the grounds on which it was adopted, is childish folly. Error is none the more sacred for having been em-braced, a lie none the more venerable for having been told.

Fickleness of opinion, apart from dishonesty, arises for the most part from an imbecility of understanding, which fluctuates between conflicting probabilities without being able to determine the preponderance. It cannot survey the question as a whole; a single view excludes every other from the horizon of its vision; as each side is successively exam-ined, each for the moment appears to be inviting. The mind vacillates and wavers. The assent oscillates from argument to argument, without the power of becoming fixed. The man is always of the last opinion which had pleaded its cause before him. He wants breadth of intel-lect, he wants the power of comparing and weighing. The forces, to borrow a physical illustration, act upon him suc-cessively and singly; he wants the power of combining and resolving them. "His second thinking only upsets the first, and his third confounds them both." The case of such a man—to use the striking illustration of Foster—"is like the case of a rustic walking in London, who, having no cer-tain direction through the vast confusion of streets to the place where he wishes to be, advances and hesitates, and turns and inquires, and becomes at each corner still more inextricably perplexed." Men of extraordinary acuteness are apt to be the victims of their own ingenuity. They see objections in the minuteness of their gaze which others of wider vision had overlooked. Straws are magnified into formidable obstacles, and mole-hills swell into mountains. Men of this sort cannot be said to have an opinion. Their assent is not stable enough to deserve the name; it is hardly more than a leaning, and hence they are ever learning and never able to arrive at the knowledge of the truth. They are only the receptacles of the various appearances of things which in succession invite their attention, and, like the chameleon, they always exhibit the colour of the last object they touch. What they call their opinions are simply copies of these successive impressions, and are as various and fluctuating as the phenomena themselves. These are the species of changes which constitute fickleness; this is real vacillation. But a change from the less to the more perfect, from error to truth, indicates neither weakness nor oscillation.

2. No more is consistency or firmness of opinion to be confounded with obstinacy. That is the creature not of evidence or the love of truth, but of stupidity or pride. It may spring from an incapacity to appreciate argument—a *vis inertiæ* of the mind—which causes it to stagnate in its present condition, and then, as Foster has happily illustrated a kindred temper, "its constancy is rather of the nature of a dead weight than of strength; resembling less the reaction of a powerful spring than the gravitation of a big stone." Or it may arise from incorrigible headiness, which prefers the reputation of consistency to that of candour, and sacrifices truth to vanity. Its decisive argument in this aspect is always personal: I have said so, or I have expressed such an opinion, and, like the law of the Medes and Persians, I cannot change. It is a blind, bold presumption of personal infallibility. The ass or the mule may be obstinate, but neither can ever be consistent. Consistency is the inflexibility of principle, obstinacy the inflexibility of pride. Reason predominates in the one, will in the other. The one is a homage to truth; the other is the idolatry of self. When obstinacy is associated with uncharitableness, it becomes bigotry. It is one of the effects of candid inquiry, accompanied as it is with a sense of the difficulties that

attend the investigation of truth, that it renders us lenient
to the weaknesses and errors of others. We may be sensible
of the mischief likely to result from perverse opinions, and
may feel the obligation of counteracting their influence, but
we learn to distinguish betwixt the sentiments and the man.
The worst doctrines excite, in relation to the individual,
only pity or compassion, though in themselves they are the
objects of a righteous abhorrence. It is not more characteristic of charity that it rejoices in the truth than it is characteristic of the love of truth that it rejoices in charity. The
consistent man, however, is by no means insensible to error.
There is a bastard liberality which conceals its indifference
under the specious pretext of thinking no evil. There is
not energy enough in its apprehensions of truth to rouse
any emotion : there is nothing that can be called love. It
is the frigid tranquillity of a mind which prefers ease to
every other good.

But as the counterpart of spurious charity (such is the
weakness of human nature) we are constantly tempted to
confound asperity of invective with zeal for truth, bitterness
of denunciation with opposition to error. We are prone to
call down fire from heaven upon those who differ from us,
forgetting that the dispensation has passed away in which
truth was civil obedience, and error rebellion against the
State. Opinions, except in cases in which they are promo-
tive of sedition or of crime, are no longer offences within the
jurisdiction of the magistrate ; and we are not at liberty to
cherish a spirit which would prompt us to persecute if persecution were still within our power. The golden mean
betwixt indifference on the one hand and intolerance on the
other is characteristic of genuine consistency. There is a
love of truth which is superior to every other consideration :
there is also, from the necessary law of contraries, a corresponding detestation of falsehood. There is also sympathy
with the weakness and prejudices of men, and a sincere desire to see the emancipation of their minds fully achieved.
The result is a mixed state in which all these elements are

fused—the exemplification of the apostolic method of speaking the truth in love. It should not be overlooked that there are occasions on which the profoundest charity employs the language of the sternest rebuke. Men must sometimes be pulled out of the fire with violence; and in such cases it is preposterous to complain of the rudeness of the means when they were the only ones that could avail. The sleeping hypocrite is not to be aroused by honeyed words, nor a shameless impostor exposed by delicate and courtly phrases. It is Charity herself that thunders the woe in their ears. It is not the language of malice, but of pity; and it is with a heavy heart and a sad countenance that he who is intent upon the best interests of his race must denounce the vengeance of God against those whom his very earnestness evinces that he is anxious to rescue from ruin. He has no pleasure in contemplating the doom he proclaims. It is not the constancy nor the zeal of the bigot and sectary which justly exposes them to contempt: it is the pride which lies at the bottom of their opinions and the malignity which pervades their spirit. They neither love truth nor their race; they are simply lovers of themselves.

There is no truth which the young are in more danger of forgetting than that genuine stability of opinion can never be obtained as the object of direct effort. To make constancy an idol is to disregard the authority of candour as the pervading law of intellectual activity. It is a foolish prejudice which hesitates to inquire because it is afraid of change. True firmness is only the result of a perpetual and persevering honesty of mind. He that always walks by the same rule need not be afraid of inconsistency. Make the love of truth the supreme principle of thought, guard against the influences which are likely to seduce you into error, love truth for itself and not for its dowry, and your path will be as the shining light which shineth more and more unto the perfect day. If at any time you have been deceived by error, do not hesitate to renounce it as soon as it is discovered. Let no pride of opinion replace candour with obstinacy, or tempt you to confound stubbornness with firmness. Be not ashamed to acknowledge that you are fallible and imperfect, but be ashamed to confess that you prefer stagnation to improvement. It was a noble answer of Melancthon, when reproached with inconsistency on account of the abandonment in later life of some of his juvenile opinions, that he would be very sorry to think that he had lived so long without learning anything. The same silly prejudice against change which tempts us to stereotype opinions is the deadly foe to all improvement in the State. Innovations are dreaded, without respect to their character and tendencies, on the naked ground that they involve a departure from established customs. Beyond doubt, a presumption is always against them; and it is far better to stand still than to introduce changes merely from the love of novelty. But society, like the individual, is certainly capable of improvement; and when it is a real "reformation that draweth on the change, and not the desire of change that pretendeth the reformation," it is a blind idolatry of the past that resists the innovation. True conservation combines stability with the spirit of progress. It retains the good, and incorporates with it whatever of utility or excellence the present has to offer. It imitates time, which, as Lord Bacon remarks, "innovateth greatly, but quietly and by degrees scarce to be perceived." It is opposed to all violent disruptions or radical revolutions; it would have the past and the future so imperceptibly blended with each other that they should run together and coalesce without an absolute commencement or a sudden termination.

As fickleness results, in a great measure, from imbecility of understanding and a want of confidence in our own judgments, it is a matter of the utmost importance that we train our minds to a military discipline of thought. There are some persons who can hardly be said to think: they are the passive recipients of impressions and suggestions derived from their circumstances or surrounding objects; but they exert no active influence upon the train which passes through their minds. They have no grasp of anything. Hence, what they call their opinions must sit loosely upon them. The least opposition or difficulty disconcerts them; they dare not rely upon themselves. The remedy against this evil is the habit, acquired by ceaseless vigilance and discipline, of thinking clearly, distinctly and coherently. The confidence in our faculties must not be a reckless presumption; this is the parent of obstinacy and conceit: it must result from the consciousness that we see things in their just proportions and survey them in their true significancy. The confidence of philosophy is always accompanied by humility and modesty. Though the man may feel that his notions are clear and connected, and entertain no distrust of any given opinion, yet there is such an habitual sense of the limitation of his faculties and of the boundless regions over which his ignorance extends that he is always modest and unassuming. Presumption, on the contrary, aspires to omniscience; it regards its faculties as competent for anything, and is prepared to assert that nothing exists beyond the territory in which its excursions have been made.

The fickleness which results from the influences of sinister motives, in which the heart is made to corrupt the head, deserves rather to be called dishonesty than fickleness. As we have already seen, belief is not wholly involuntary. We can mould our opinions into the type of our passions and our interests. A sophist may finally succeed in persuading his understanding to embrace any lie. When interest, or ambition, or the love of pleasure, is stronger than the love of truth, we may expect a man to reflect, in the variety of his opinions, the variety of shapes which these objects are accustomed to assume. This is, perhaps, the most fruitful source of the changes in principle which distinguish those who court popular favour. They trim their sails to the breeze. In some instances they are flagrantly dishonest— they profess opinions which they do not believe—but in many others they are the dupes of their passions. They have revolved the desirableness of change so long and earnestly that they finally experience it. It is this species of fickleness which the moral sense of mankind so indignantly condemns. We can pity the man who vacillates because he is incapable of vigorous and systematic thought; but the man who changes his opinions with his interests, who inquires only for the expedient and not for the true, who is more solicitous about what shall serve a turn than what is conducive to the health of his understanding or the good of his kind, we despise too much to pity. The baseness of such conduct, and the moral resentment which every ingenuous mind cherishes against it, bring all change into suspicion. Men seek consistency for itself in order to escape the odium of sinister and selfish motives. They feel that the imputation of dishonesty may be cast upon them, and are afraid to confess their errors and follow the course of their sincere and unbiassed convictions.

The only antidote to this species of inconsistency is to be found in that moral and religious culture which gives the law of God and the authority of conscience the supremacy to which they are entitled. We must expel unhallowed motives by the operation of others of an opposite character; the devils must be ejected by fasting and prayer. It is a corrupt and deceitful nature which occasions the mischief, and a complete exemption can only be secured by the renovation of the soul. The fountain must be purified, the tree made good, or no thorough reformation can take place. No man is safe from the danger of tergiversation and apostasy as long as any principle obtains in his heart stronger than the fear of God. There is always a point, like the heel of Achilles, in which he is vulnerable.

II. Closely allied to stability of opinion is consistency or harmony of life. When a man's actions correspond to his professed principles, and fulfil the expectations which his character and past conduct have excited, he is entitled to the distinction of a consistent man. "His carriage is conformable to itself." The standard of virtuous consistency is the pervading influence of integrity of heart. He whose eye is single will never be wayward in his course.

Inconsistency may spring from a defect of understanding, which grasps its principles too loosely to give them an operative influence upon the conduct, or from defect of will, which is not able to resist the temptations to a contrary course, or from defect of honesty in professing principles which one does not actually believe. The first is fickleness, the second weakness, and the third hypocrisy.

1. In the first case, the principles may be sound and upright, but as they have no hold upon the heart the springs of action are independent of them as to the influences which excite and the motives which regulate their course. The man is as completely the creature of impulse as if he were destitute of reason or of conscience. This want of energy in the understanding is a very different thing from impotency of will. The principles *would* control if the man had a firm hold upon them, but his notions are superficial, his thoughts without intensity, his mind is languid and sleepy. He rather dozes over his principles than believes them. As there is a torpor of the imagination which often renders a man rude and repulsive through inability to exchange situations with another, and realize his own feelings upon the change, so every one must have noticed that the intellectual operations of some men are so lifeless and inert that for all practical purposes they might almost as well be without an understanding at all. Such men when required to act are like a ship without a rudder, exposed to the mercy of the winds and waves. Their impulses are apt to be in the inverse ratio of their mental energy, and hence their conduct may be expected to exhibit all the fluctuations and caprices of passion and appetite. The explanation of their waywardness is not that they have no principles, but that their principles want intensity; they are on the surface, not in the texture, of the soul.

2. By defect of will, in the second case, I mean a defect in strength of purpose. There are sound principles, and

there is a general resolution to exemplify them in life, but upon occasions of sudden temptation, or where the inducements to transgression are strong and multiplied, the will is mastered. In this case there is no torpor; there are life and activity, there is often a severe, sometimes a protracted conflict, and the will seldom yields until the understanding has been bribed into a lie. But still, as the seat of the disorder is in the active principles of our nature, and as the temptation is immediately addressed to them, this species of inconsistency may be ascribed to the state of the will. This is the kind of inconsistency that most generally prevails in the world. The changes of fortune from adversity to prosperity or from prosperity to adversity, from honour to shame or from contempt to popularity, from poverty to wealth or from wealth to poverty; the changes of situation from a public to a private or from a private to a public station; our different circumstances and relations; the different societies into which we are thrown,—are so many trials of the strength of virtue, and few have been able to undergo them without tripping in their steps. To keep the even tenor of one's way in sunshine and storm, through evil as well as through good report, amid afflictions and reproaches as well as smiles and benedictions, is a proof of integrity which he is thrice blessed who can appropriate to himself. To be always the same, at all times, in all places, in all conditions, in all companies; to stand firmly by our principles at every sacrifice of interest or of fame; to consent to be misunderstood and maligned rather than let go our integrity; to count nothing a good but duty, nothing ill but wrong,—this is a perfection of character which, while it is incumbent upon all to pursue, such is the melancholy weakness of human nature that it has never been realized but once. Our efforts are at best but faint approximations. We press forward; we have not already attained, but the prize is in view. We have but one rule to go by. The law of the Lord must be in our hearts, must be the controlling law of our wills, if we would keep us from the paths of the destroyer. When the principles of duty are habits, and holiness is the nature of the soul, then, and then only, can we hope to be perfect. But in the mean time our duty is to watch against temptation, and pray for strength to resist it. Vigilance and prayer are the indispensable conditions of success. Let no man presume upon his own strength. The stoutest have fallen, and though low and vulgar temptations may have no effect upon us, yet depend upon it that there is some door by which every heart can be entered unless kept by the Keeper of Israel, and betrayed into the hands of the enemy. No man is safe but he who abides under the shadow of the Almighty. Of every other it may be truly said that he stands " in slippery places," and his " feet shall slide in due time."

3. The third case of inconsistency is an instance of pure hypocrisy, and, after what has already been said of the law of sincerity, requires no other notice than that of stern and indignant reprobation.

The conduct of men in relation to religion is chargeable with inconsistency in all these aspects. In the first place, they assent to its doctrines; they acknowledge its overwhelming importance—that it is the one thing needful, and should constitute the great absorbing business of their lives; they profess to be convinced of truths which it would seem are enough to shake heaven and earth in the great commotion; and yet so little power do these principles have upon their minds that hardly a trace of their influence can be detected in the daily walk. They receive only a cold and otiose assent; all living interest is expended upon the world. Again, when the conscience has been really awakened, and the sinner is aroused to some effort for the salvation of the soul, how feeble and irresolute are the decisions of the will! The truth is felt, but the lusts of the flesh are stronger than it, and, unless grace interpose, in every instance secure the victory. What is still worse, the transgressor, as a quietus to his conscience, sometimes assumes the obligations of religion, and undertakes to palm upon his God the form as a substitute for the substance. We have all dealt faithlessly upon this subject. We have resisted reason, conscience and the Spirit of God. We have been wayward and rebellious children. Let us resolve, in all future time, to act in accordance with the dignity of rational and intellectual beings. If religion is *true*, let us embrace it in our hearts and embody it in our lives. If there is an endless destiny for which we are called to prepare, let us project our plans upon a scale commensurate with its grandeur, and pursue them to their consummation with untiring zeal and perseverance. Let us fix our eyes upon the skies, and in seeking glory, honour and immortality we shall assuredly lay hold upon eternal life. Supreme devotion to the glory of God will give consistency to our thoughts and harmony to our lives. *I have set the Lord always before me: because He is at my right hand, I shall not be moved.*[1]

III. Before concluding this discourse it may not be improper, though the subject is only remotely connected with that of truth, to make a few remarks upon that species of consistency which obtains in the correspondence of our actions to our external circumstances and incidental relations. This is properly decorum or decency. In a wide sense decency covers the whole ground of our relations, and includes the dignity of virtue as well as the proprieties of life. There is an intimate alliance, no doubt, between integrity of heart and a delicate refinement of manners. Each adorns its possessor; each is beautiful and lovely. The two combined make up that gracefulness of character which Cicero so warmly commends in his Offices. Whatever is virtuous is certainly becoming—it is adapted to the nature and state of the species; and it should be an additional incentive to duty that it not only contributes to the health but to the ornament and glory of man. In the sight of angels and of holy beings the sinner is a deformed and ugly thing; his habits and affections are as unsuited to the constitution of his mind as coarse and unseemly apparel or rude

[1] Ps. xvi. 8.

and boisterous manners to a festival or a court. They contemplate him with feelings analogous to those with which
we contemplate the disgusting coarseness of the low and
abandoned. The disproportion betwixt his faculties and
actions, betwixt his capacities and ends, is so huge and
revolting that we can well understand the terms of self-
loathing and abhorrence, of shame and confusion of face,
which true penitence is accustomed to appropriate. And of
all indecencies impiety is the most monstrous. It is an outrage upon the original dignity of man—a being made but
little less than the angels and capable of eating angels' food—
to waste his noble energies upon the beggarly elements of
earth. It is a lamentation, and shall be for a lamentation,
that he who might aspire to communion and fellowship with
God should be content to accept his portion among the beasts
that perish. Religion is the true glory of man, and those
who despise its claims must, from the necessity of the case,
awake to shame and everlasting contempt.

But my purpose, at present, is not to discuss the fitnesses
which grow out of the essential relations of humanity, all-
important as these are, and interesting as is the light in
which they hold up the beauty and dignity of virtue. I
now have in view those external and incidental relations
which are peculiar to individuals, and which grow out of
their age, station, business and pursuits. Cicero has marked
the distinction and given some admirable hints for preserv-
ing decorum in each. What is becoming in the young is
not becoming in the old; what is becoming in a servant
might not be becoming in his master; what is suited to the
condition of a peasant would be grossly out of proportion to
the state of a lord. The rules which custom has sanctioned
are not altogether arbitrary. They are founded upon an
analogy which is much more easily felt than defined; and
delicacy of sensibility to this species of decency is the mark
of a noble and generous mind. It is what is commonly
called, especially when associated with solid virtue, dignity
of character. This was the kind of fitness which Themis-

tocles had his eye on when he rebutted the imputation growing out of his want of a common accomplishment: " I cannot fiddle, but I know how to make a small town a great city." It was not for a man whose mind was intent upon grand and lofty aims to be stooping to the amusements of the giddy and the gay. This same spirit was exemplified in Nehemiah when he indignantly rejected an unworthy proposal : " And I said, Should such a man as I flee? and who is there that, being as I am, would go into the temple to save his life? I will not go in."[1] In contrast to these cases is the conduct of Nero fiddling when Rome was on fire, and disguised as a charioteer when an atrocious persecution was going on. The life of the bloody Jeffreys is not more distinguished by the savage depravity of his heart, and the prostitution of his office to the most wicked and corrupt designs, than by the brutal ferocity of his manners and the degradation of his rank by the most shameful and revolting indecencies. He had as little sense of decorum as of duty.

There may be refinement of external manners and scrupulous attention to outward decorum as the results of education and habit without sensibility to beauty and without moral culture. Accomplishments may be mechanically imparted and mechanically used. But in these cases they are cold and repulsive. They want the freshness and glow of nature and of life. They are truly graceful only when they are the genuine expressions of the spirit of the mind. He, therefore, that would aspire to the praise of dignity of character must study at once the general excellence of his nature and his particular sphere as an individual. He must aim at worth as a man, and at propriety as such a man. He must cherish a nice discernment of the beautiful and becoming, and not permit himself to become familiar with the little, the degrading and the mean.

It is in their relaxations and amusements that men are most apt to forget what is due to their character. When

[1] Neh. vi. 11.

the eye of the world is upon them, or when they are engaged in their pursuits of business, they are not so likely to unbend. But in their hours of recreation they not unfrequently compound with their dignity. This is particularly the case with the young at that most important period of their lives when they are laying the foundations of their future characters. Colleges and universities, both in this country and Europe, have suffered from no cause more severely than inattention on the part of their students to what was due to the station they occupy. The indecency of their amusements has been the bane of these seats of learning, and has counteracted the effect in multiplied instances of the most faithful instruction. Antecedently to experience we should form a fine picture of a youthful student; we should figure him as one whose mind was expanding in knowledge, who was beginning to taste the sweetness of truth, to relish the beautiful and admire the good. We should expect him to be animated with a just sense of the dignity of his pursuits, to breathe their refinement, and to reflect in all his conversation and deportment the elevating influence of letters. His amusements and recreations, we should naturally think, would be impregnated with the same spirit. The groves in which he would walk, the place in which he would dwell, we should spontaneously image to our fancy as the abodes of quiet, tranquillity and peace. But how sadly are these anticipations too often disappointed! "Let him," says the biographer of Bacon, "who is fond of indulging in dreamlike existence, go to Oxford and stay there; let him study this magnificent spectacle, the same under all aspects, with its mental twilight tempering the glare of noontide or mellowing the shadowy moonlight; let him wander in her sylvan suburbs or linger in her cloistered halls, but let him not catch the din of scholars or teachers, or dine or sup with them, or speak a word to any of the privileged inhabitants, for if he does, the spell will be broken, the poetry and the religion gone, and the palace of enchantment will melt from his

embrace into thin air." If the vain and frivolous agita-
tions of their wit were all that disfigured our seats of learning,
the evil would not be so intolerable. But how ill do tur-
bulence, riot and disorder, boisterous mirth, coarse ribaldry,
and even open profanity, comport with the temple which
has been consecrated to letters! The case is immeasurably
worse when a low standard of opinion endures, if it does
not sanction, flagrant breaches of morality. It is the influence of these abuses which in too many cases has rendered
public schools and colleges, in the language of Dr. Arnold,
"nurseries of vice." "Those who are dismissed from the
parental roof," complains the same illustrious teacher,
"frank, open, ingenuous and pure, soon lose these graces
which adorn them, and return, to their parents' shame, without modesty, without nice sensibility to truth, without tenderness and sympathy, coarse, false and unfeeling." This
is the natural result of departing in the first instance from
the spirit of rigid propriety. *Proficere in pejus* is the law
of degradation. When the general feeling of fitness is
shocked or rudely disregarded, a man has taken a step towards
the corruption of his principles as well as his manners. The
sentiment of honour is weakened by every blow which is
inflicted on the sense of propriety. He that becomes accustomed to what is unseemly and unbecoming, and out of all
proportion in lighter matters, will soon lose the perception
of the beautiful in the weightier matters of the law. This
is the reason why it is so important that the amusements of
the young should be made to harmonize with their condition and relations. In these amusements a moral discipline
is going on—a moral influence exerted which will tell upon
their future character. Unconsciously but surely they are
shaping their destiny.

Many of these inconsistencies, my young friends, I rejoice
to say cannot be imputed to you. They are of a character
to make you scorn them. But be not satisfied with present
attainments. Let it be your ambition to have a college in

which the deportment of every member shall reflect the refinement of the gentleman, the dignity of the scholar and the integrity of the Christian. We can make this a delightful place, we can turn these groves into hallowed ground, and these cloistered halls we can render worthy of the illustrious immortals who linger among them in their works. Is not this an object worthy of your ambition? Here we are permitted to converse from day to day with the sages, poets and heroes of antiquity: " the blind old man of Scio's rocky isle;" that prodigy of genius, whose birth-place was Stagira, whose empire has been the world; that other prodigy of common sense who brought wisdom from the skies, the divine Plato; the masters of the Porch, Academy and Lyceum, are all here. Here, too, we can listen to the rapt visions of the prophets, hold converse with apostles and martyrs, and, above all, sit at the feet of Him who spake as never man spake. Here, in a single word, we are " let into that great communion of scholars throughout all ages and all nations, like that more awful communion of saints in the Holy Church Universal, and feel a sympathy with departed genius, and with the enlightened and gifted minds of other countries as they appear before us in the transports of a sort of beatific vision, bowing down at the same shrines and glowing with the same holy love of whatever is most pure, and fair, and exalted, and divine in human nature." Is there nothing in such society and such influences to stimulate our minds to a lofty pitch? Catch the spirit of the place, imbibe its noble associations, and you cannot descend to the little, the trifling, the silly or the coarse. Every fibre of your hearts would cry out against it. When Bonaparte animated his troops in Egypt it was enough to point to the Pyramids, beneath whose shadows they stood, and say, " From yonder heights forty generations look down upon you." That thought was enough. The same great motive may be applied to you. The general assembly of the great, and good, and learned, and glorious of all ages and of all climes look down upon *you* and exhort you to walk worthy of your exalted calling. Quit yourselves like men, and make this venerable seat of learning a joy and a praise in all the earth. Let TRUTH be inscribed on its walls, TRUTH worshipped in its sanctuary, and the LOVE OF TRUTH the inspiration of every heart.

INDEX

A

AMS, Dr. Jaspar, 102

STOTLE, 10, 28, 29, 82

NOLD, Dr. 159

GUSTIN, 77, 128

B

CON, Lord, 4, 34, 149

IEF, responsibility of men to, 25, 27, 40

OTRY, 146, 148

OUGHMAN, Lord, 37

TLER, Bishop, 19, 30, 40

C

VIN, 121, 122, 124, 129

ARITY, true distinguished from ious, 147

RIST, the Truth, 27

RISTIAN, model character, 2, 3

ERO, 10, 40, 91, 155, 156

RKE, Samuel, 40

MMUNION WITH GOD, as the source of iness, 9, 13

NSCIENCE, relation of to the underling, 30-32; moral judgment an element in decisions, 31; laws of rectitude in the lative and constitutive principles of duty, aws of the, applied by the understanding to rete cases, 31; affected by the Fall, 31.

NSCIOUSNESS, primary data of the dard and measure of evidence, 49-51; two s in which we may be misled as to the ary data of, 51.

CONSISTENCY, discourse on, 142-161; definition of, 142-144; in relation to truth is constancy, 144; as involving stability of opinion, 144-151; as involving harmony of life, 151-155; as involving a correspondence of actions to circumstances and relations, 155-159

CONTROVERSY, mode of conducting, 60

CUDWORTH, 40

D

DECORUM, as involving the correspondence of actions to circumstances and relations, 155-159

DENS' THEOLOGY, 68

DEPRAVITY, doctrine of the Scriptures as to, 18

DICK, DR. JOHN, 80

DISCIPLINE, of thought necessary, 149, 150

DUTY, taught with certainty in the Scriptures, 7-9

E

EQUIVOCATION, 84,85

EVIDENCE, the only measure of assent to professed truth, a great principle, 49-60

F

FAITHFULNESS, discourse on, 91-116; definition of, 91,92; in relation to promises, 92-106; in relation to pledges, 106-112; of God in fulfillment of His promises, 105,106.

FALSEHOOD, speculative, fatal to moral integrity, 33-36.

FICKLENESS, of opinion, 145, 146, 149-151; of opinion, antidote to, 151; of life, 152.

FICTIONS, law of truth as applied to, 79.

FLATTERY, 83.

FOSTER, JOHN, 145

FREEDOM, consistency of, with obligation to obey God, 125, 126.

FRENCH ENCYCLOPAEDISTS, their mode of treating Christianity, 65.

FRIENDSHIP, pretensions to as an evasion truth, 83, 84.

G

GOD, faithfulness of, in the fulfillment of His promises, 105, 106; communion with, the source of true happiness, 12, 13.

GRACES, distinction between and moral habits, 21.

H

HALL, BISHOP, 122.

HAMILTON, SIR W., 28.

HAPPINESS, doctrine of the Scriptures as to, 10-15; Aristotle's doctrine of, 10, 11, 12; defect of Paley's doctrine as to, 14.

HARMONY OF LIFE, as correspondence of actions to professed porinciples, 151-155.

HOLINESS, doctrine of the Scriptures as to, 15-20; definition of, 16; the all-pervading condition of spiritual action, 17.

HOWE, JOHN, 14, 15.

HYPOCRISY, characteristics of, 82, 83; a cause of inconsistency of life, 154.

I

IMPULSES, BLIND, what, 25.

INCONSISTENCY OF LIFE, causes of, 152-155; in relation to religion, 154, 155.

J

JOHNSON, SAMUEL, 118.

K

KANT, 31.

KNOWLEDGE, essential to moral culture, 32; relative and phenomenal, 45; pursuit universal, not incumbent on all, 45, 46; of Go Christ, the duty of all who have the Scriptures,

L

LANGUAGE, origin of, 72, 73

LAWS OF BELIEF, guides to the understan in the pursuit of the truth, 49-51.

LIBERALITY, false, 599.

LIES, nature of, 70, 71, 77, 86-88; lawfulnes for concealment, discussed, 81, 82; justifia ness of, discussed, 86-90.

LIFE, difficulty of comprehending, 17; all vading condition of action, 17.

LOCKE, 48, 49, 53.

LOT, The, indiscriminate use of, 135

LOVE TO GOD, the fundamental princip holiness, 17

M

MACKINTOSH, SIR J., 37.

MELANCTHON, 149.

MENTAL RESERVATIONS, 85

MORALITY, natural systems of, defectiv two respects, 5,6; domain of, co-extensive whole nature of man, 25.

MORAL OBLIGATION, tampering with principles of, the worst form of wickedness, 3

N

NATURE, as, what, 16

O

OBLIGATION, to obey God consistent freedom, 125, 126

OBSTINACY, not to be confounded with sistency, 146; the causes, 146

NION, responsibility as to, 36-40

P

LEY, 6, 7, 10, 14, 64, 70, 78, 86, 88, 96, 97, , 112, 132.

RABLE, the law of truth as applied to the, 78

RCEPTION, mistake of philosophers as to, centuries, 53

RJURY, peculiar enormity of, 134, 135, 139

ILOSOPHY, moral, contradistinguished n man's moral constitution, 6, 7; inability of, define holiness, 15, 16; dumb, as to the readment of man's judicial relations to God, 120; nility and modesty of true, 150

ATONISTS, THE, rules for purgation of the l, 58

EDGES, definition of, 86, 87; guilt of break-, 107-109; God's use of, in the Gospel, 111,

EJUDICE, influence of, on the pursuit of th, 54-59

ESUMPTION, rebuke of, 150

OFANITY, enormous guilt of, 134-136

OMISES, nature of, 70, 92-97; grounds of igation of, 97-100; question as to binding ure of, extorted, 100, 101; effect of unlawful ditions upon the validity of, 101-105; of God, the Gospel, 105, 106; distinction between arent and real, 94; cautions against indiscreet, -116

R

ASON, question of sufficiency of, in morals,

DEMPTION, relation of, to ethics, 8-23; a ine institute of holiness, 22

GENERATION, necessity of, 21

D, THOMAS, 76

VELATION, necessity of, exaggerated, 4

REYNOLDS, BISHOP, 122

ROME, CHURCH OF, difference between, and Protestants as to the estimate of vows, 117, 118

S

SCHLEIERMACHER, 18

SCOTT, SIR W., his concealment of the authorship of the Waverly Novels, 81

SCRIPTURES, THE, ethical system of expounded, 1-23; sufficiency of, as a rule of duty, 6-23; are an answer to the questions of ancient philosophy, 10; doctrine of, as to happiness, 10-15; doctrine of, as to holiness, 15-20; doctrine of, as to the mode of accomplishing the end of our being, 20-22; doctrine of, as to the extent of the rule of conscience, 25;.

SHAME, influence of, upon the pursuit of truth, 63-65

SILENCE, law of truth as applied to, 80

SIN, effect of the first, on the transgressor, 18, 19; influence of each act of, upon the moral constitution, 107-109

SINCERITY, as an element of practical truth, 76-90; definition of, 67-69; duties involved in the law of, 76, 82; application of law of, to parables, fictions, etc., 78, 79; application of law of, to feigned action, 78-80; law of, as to silence contemplating concealment, 80, 81; law of, as to direct falsehoods contemplating concealment, 78-80; modes in which the law of, is evaded, 82-85; hypocrisy as an evasion of the law of, 82, 83; flattery as an evasion of the law of, 83; false pretensions to friendship as an evasion of the law of, 83, 84; equivocation as an evasion of the law of, 84, 85; mental reservation as an evasion of the law of, 85.

SKEPTICISM, origin and nature of, 51, 53

SOPHISTRY, in speculation is hypocrisy in practice, 36.

SOUTH, DR., 71, 77.

STABILITY OF OPINION, an element of consistency, 144-151; consistency of, with change implied in legitimate progress, 144-146;

difference between, and obstinacy, 146-148; not the result of direct effort, 148

SUPEREROGATION, impossibility of works of, 127; hurtfulness of the doctrine of, 127

T

TAYLOR, JEREMY, 100, 123, 127

THEMISTOCLES, 156, 157

TRUTH, discourses on, 1-161; the love of, 24-66; a law for the conduct of the understanding, 26, 27; the food of the soul, 27, 28; the invigorator of the mind, 28, 29; a variable standard of, as affecting morals, 31; love of, as a general habit of the mind, 35, 36; love of, as a duty, 40; love of, as beautiful, 41; the great end of intellectual effort, 41; love of, as a safeguard against temptation, 42; love of, precludes prejudice, 47-49; evidence the measure of assent to professed, 49-60; fundamental laws of belief as guides in pursuit of, 49-51; pursuit of, as affected by prejudice, 54-58; love of, injured by arguing on side of a question known to be wrong, 60; love of, as affected by vanity, 60-63; love of, as affected by shame, 63-66; two leading aspects of, speculative and practical, 67; practical, considered, 67-161; practical, involves the three elements of sincerity, faithfulness and consistency, 67-70; grounds of obligation of, 70-76; origin of, natural not conventional, 75; two principles of practical, underlying social intercourse, 75, 76; not restricted to speech, 77; justifiableness of evasions of, 86-90.

U

UNDERSTANDING, THE, effect of, when blind, on morals, 31-34; not exempt from the authority of the will, 36-40; subject to the control of conscience, 26-40; evidence the measure of assent, the great law for conduct, 58.

V

VANITY, influence of, upon the pursuit of truth, 60-63

VERACITY, definition of, 68; matter of it, 68, 69; grounds of obligation of, 70-76; Paley's and South's views as to the obligation of, discussed, 70-73; Whewell's views as to the obligation of, discussed, 72-75; real ground of obligation 75, 76

VIRTUE, distinction between elicit and imper acts of, 122

VOSSIUS, 93

VOWS, discourse on, 117-141; differe between Protestants and Romanist estimates 117, 118; nature of, 118-125; uses of, 125-1 obligation of, 131-141; are of the general nat of promises, 118, 119; are made to God, 1 120; are of the nature of oaths, 120; spirit which they ought to be made, 120, 121; religid should respect acts appointed in God's word, l other, should respect either elicit or imperate of some virtue, 122; as to matter, should be in power, 123; of consecration and thanksgivi 124; hurtfulness of, made in a mercenary sp 126; usefulness of, regarded as possessing mi 126; proper, are helps to piety, 128-130; Calvi view of the four ends of, 129; evil effect making them common, 130, 131; Paley's the as to obligation of promises applied to, 132, l true ground of obligation of, 133, 134; g involved in violation of, 134-138; forgotten unredeemed, 139-161.

W

WATTS, ISAAC, 24, 98.

WHEWELL, PROFESSOR, 73, 102.

WILL, THE, moral relation of, to our bl impulses, 26; as controlling the intellect operations, 36-40; influence of each act upon character, 107-109; weakness of, a cause inconsistency of life, 152-154.

WOLLISTON, 40.

WORKS, dead and wicked, compared, 21.

Other Solid Ground Titles

In addition to *Whatsoever Things are True* which you hold in your hand, Solid Ground is honored to offer many other uncovered treasure, many for the first time in more than a century:

LET THE CANNON BLAZE AWAY by Joseph P. Thompson
THE STILL HOUR: *Communion with God in Prayer* by Austin Phelps
COLLECTED WORKS of James Henley Thornwell (4 vols.)
CALVINISM IN HISTORY *by Nathaniel S. McFetridge*
OPENING SCRIPTURE: *Hermeneutical Manual by Patrick Fairbairn*
THE ASSURANCE OF FAITH *by Louis Berkhof*
THE PASTOR IN THE SICK ROOM *by John D. Wells*
THE BUNYAN OF BROOKLYN: *Life & Sermons of I.S. Spencer*
THE NATIONAL PREACHER: Sermons from 2nd Great Awakening
FIRST THINGS: First Lessons God Taught Mankind *Gardiner Spring*
BIBLICAL & THEOLOGICAL STUDIES *by 1912 Faculty of Princeton*
THE POWER OF GOD UNTO SALVATION *by B.B. Warfield*
THE LORD OF GLORY *by B.B. Warfield*
A GENTLEMAN & A SCHOLAR: *Memoir of J.P. Boyce by J. Broadus*
SERMONS TO THE NATURAL MAN *by W.G.T. Shedd*
SERMONS TO THE SPIRITUAL MAN *by W.G.T. Shedd*
HOMILETICS AND PASTORAL THEOLOGY *by W.G.T. Shedd*
A PASTOR'S SKETCHES 1 & 2 *by Ichabod S. Spencer*
THE PREACHER AND HIS MODELS *by James Stalker*
IMAGO CHRISTI *by James Stalker*
A HISTORY OF PREACHING *by Edwin C. Dargan*
LECTURES ON THE HISTORY OF PREACHING *by J. A. Broadus*
THE SCOTTISH PULPIT *by William Taylor*
THE SHORTER CATECHISM ILLUSTRATED *by John Whitecross*
THE CHURCH MEMBER'S GUIDE *by John Angell James*
THE SUNDAY SCHOOL TEACHER'S GUIDE *by John A. James*
CHRIST IN SONG: *Hymns of Immanuel from All Ages by Philip Schaff*
COME YE APART: *Daily Words from the Four Gospels by J.R. Miller*
DEVOTIONAL LIFE OF THE S.S. TEACHER *by J.R. Miller*

Call us Toll Free at 1-877-666-9469
Send us an e-mail at sgcb@charter.net
Visit us on line at solid-ground-books.com

Uncovering Buried Treasure to the Glory of God

CPSIA information can be obtained at www.ICGtesting.com
Printed in the USA
LVOW120455300312

275348LV00001B/25/A